The Italian Crooners Bedside Companion

By Richard Grudens

Foreword by Jerry Vale

The Italian Crooners Bedside Companion

By Richard Grudens

Author of:

The Best Damn Trumpet Player
The Song Stars
The Music Men
Jukebox Saturday Night
Snootie Little Cutie - The Connie Haines Story
Jerry Vale - A Singer's Life
Magic Moments - The Sally Bennett Story
The Spirit of Bob Hope
Bing Crosby - Crooner of the Century
Chattanooga Choo Choo - The Life and Times of the
World Famous Glenn Miller Orchestra

Celebrity Profiles Publishing Company
Box 344
Stonybrook, New York 11790-0344
(631) 862-8555 Phone
(631) 862-0139 Fax
www.richardgrudens.com

Published by:
Celebrity Profiles Publishing Company
Div. Edison & Kellogg
Box 344
Stonybrook, New York 11790-0344
(631) 862-8555 Phone
(631) 862-0139 Fax
Email: celebpro4@aol.com
www.richardgrudens.com

Edited by Madeline Grudens

ISBN: 0-9763877-0-0

Printed in the United States of America

Table of Contents

PART ONE
The Great Ones

PART TWO

PART THREE
THE NEWER FELLERS

PART FOUR
SPECIAL FEATURES

PART FIVE
HONORABLE MENTIONS

THE ITALIAN BANDLEADERS

THE FAMOUS COPA BONNET

Only the really great are entitled to wear the Copa's symbol of success. It's the Night Club Academy Award... the Laurel Wreath of Stardom. Just look at the talented stars who have worn the Bonnet:

1	Jimmy Durante
2	Dean Martin
3	Dionne Warwick
4	Joe E. Lewis
5	Johnny Mathis
6	Frank Sinatra
7	Danny Thomas
8	Tony Bennett
9	Peggy Lee
10	Steve Lawrence
11	Sammy Davis, Jr.
12	Joey Bishop
14	Diana Ross and The Supremes
15	Eydie Gorme
16	Bobby Darin
17	Jerry Lewis
18	Don Rickles
19	Jerry Vale
20	Connie Francis
21	Tom Jones
22	Paul Anka

THE CAPTIVATING, SCINTILLATING COPA! This is where it all happens . . . the glitter of sparkling entertainment . . . the fun and excitement of "anything goes". . . the electricity that makes the Copa "The Great American Night Club". The Copa —inventor of what's best in cafe entertainment, hands you the evening filled with the most dance-able music in town . . . the most star-strewn musical revues East of Broadway . . . and a night to remember!

THE GREAT COPA SHOW Where else but the world-famous Copa would such unbelievable talents perform for your entertainment pleasure? No where else—because the Copa is the showcase for the stars. The biggest stars can and do call the Copa home —stars like those illustrated above—like the one you'll see tonight . . . holders of the famed Copa bonnet . . . recipients of the world's acclaim. They're all here for your enjoyment. Watch and see for yourself!

Foreword

Dear Reader,

Ever since Richard Grudens put together the story of my own wondrous career "A Singer's Life" in 2001, we have talked about the publication of this account of my fellow performers, sometimes known as *crooners*.

Whenever I fly East to perform a show or visit my daughter and grandson, Richard and I get together, usually at a radio show or a bookstore or restaurant book signing. Well, this book, The Italian Crooners Bedside Companion, is a book we have talked about for some time. It is a series of vignettes filled with interesting stories and facts about all your favorite Italian singers, and I consider myself very fortunate to be a contributor.

Many of the subjects here, are or have been, my personal friends. Tony Bennett has been a friend for many years. In my opinion, Tony is a great star and deserves all the accolades he has earned. I'm happy to call him my 'Buddy.'

And, I have always been a fan of my friend Perry Como, "Mr Class," as he has always been called by his fellow performers and countless fans. I have always tried to be just like Perry Como, as many of us have.

And what about the great Frankie Laine, who hailed from Chicago, and who sang all his great songs: "Mule Train," "Lucky Old Sun," and "That's My Desire," Who sings better than Frank, and for so many years? He celebrated his 92nd birthday last March.

Of course, Frank Sinatra is certainly in a special class. He too was a good friend and a great guy. We spent many hours together doing the things friends do; having dinner, playing cards and sharing stories. Thank God for all the wonderful music he left for us to hear. Through his countless recordings, he will always be with us, and I will always remember him as the premier performer of all the great songs.

You will find Julius La Rosa here. You will read about Al Martino and Vic Damone, Alan Dale and Johnny Desmond, Buddy Greco and Bobby Darin - yes, Bobby was Italian too. They are all here for you to read and learn about. So read on and enjoy all the stories and ups and downs of all those Italian Singers we love.

Richard has even remembered my old friend Jimmy Durante, who wasn't exactly a crooner, but he could deliver a great song too.

Jerry Vale (Genero Louis Vitaliano)
Palm Desert, California
November, 2004

Frank Sinatra

Don Cornell

Tony Bennett

Jerry Vale

Frankie Laine

Dean Martin

Jimmy Roselli

Bobby Darin

Al Martino

Julius La Rosa

Perry Como

Vic Damone

Introduction

Ciao, music lovers. This book comprises many of my personal interviews and collected works captured over a period of 35 years with the great and passionate Italian Crooners and have appeared in books, magazines and entertainment newsletters. These include the voices of Jerry Vale, Frankie Laine, Tony Bennett, Al Martino, Julius La Rosa, Dean Martin, Frank Sinatra, Perry Como, Buddy Greco, Louis Prima, Bobby Darin, Don Cornell, Jimmy Roselli, Vic Damone, Russ Columbo, Lou Monte, Jimmy Durante, Johnny Desmond, Alan Dale, Sergio Franchi, John Pizzerelli, John Primerano, Tony B. (Babino), Filippo Voltaggio, and Roberto Tirado, with a foreword by premier Italian recording artist Jerry Vale, some words of music wisdom by my mentor and good friend for over 30 years, Frankie Laine, who is 92 years young at this writing, and an introduction by Italian Music Radio host Luisa Potenza of Long Island's WALK whose radio program showcases each at his best and features personal interviews.

The book covers personal aspects of each crooner's career, many in their own words and from the lips of friends and counterparts, as well as lists of recordings, accomplishments, and displays of rare photos obtained from personal collections.

It is amazing how many Crooners have performed on the American scene, beginning around the 1920s through 2003, a memorable 83 years. The parents of these crooners had emigrated to the United States, beginning in the 1880s through the 1920s, mostly from Southern Italy and the nearby island of Sicily.

Apparently, at that time, Northern Italians scorned Southern Italians, and development of improved civilization in the South was ignored by government, and a harsh economic depression there further encouraged it's citizens to seek hope of a better life across the ocean in far-off America. Citizens had little prospects or hope for recovering from earthquakes, volcanic eruptions, and, as a result, devastating epidemics of cholera, as well as the absence of industrialization to provide needed employment. So, they came to America.

Actually, only a handful of popular crooners have not been Italian - most noticeably Bing Crosby and Nat "King Cole." And, of course, you may count out non-Italians Rudy Vallee, Mel Torme, Johnny Mathis, Herb Jeffries, Billy Eckstine, Bob Eberly and Ray Eberle, Steve Lawrence, Eddie Fisher, Jack Jones and Andy Williams, good singers, all. Many of them, however, owe thanks to the Italian singers whom they followed.

This book, unlike my earlier 1998 "Music Men," a book about_ *all* the male singers, will relate the story exclusively of only the Italian popular singers we have all enjoyed and loved.
Today, there remains a number of worthy Italian crooners on the scene, namely Frankie Laine, Jerry Vale, Tony Bennett, Al Martino, Julius La Rosa, Buddy Greco, Jimmy Roselli, Vic Damone, Bill Farrell, Frankie Sinatra, and the up-and-coming voices of Tony Babino, John Primerano, Filippo Voltaggio, Tom Postilio, Michael Bublé, and Peter Cincotti, to name a few.

Read on. The Italian Crooners Bedside Companion will keep you warm on those cold nights and cool on those hot nights with myriad memories to share.

It's all about the music and the voices that carry it to our ears.

Richard Grudens, October 2004

Our Italian Crooners

It has been my pleasure and a source of intense pride to host the weekly radio show, Italia Mia, aired on WALK radio 1370 AM. It is certainly an added pleasure to comment here on Richard Grudens' book showcasing the Italian singers who appear on my program. The show and the book are geared to Italians and Italian-Americans and is comprised of interviews, current news from Italy, an occasional cooking segment and a salute to a different region of Italy. Dom De Luise is a frequent guest on my show and is a guest here in this book, as well.

Introducing the singers of old and the new affords me great satisfaction. Requests for all-time favorites like Jerry Vale, Jimmy Roselli and Al Martino, as well as the enduring artists of yesteryear, Carlo Buti, Aurelio Fierro, Emilio Pericoli and Claudio Villa, continue to come in. Each song they sing evokes a memory of the past.

Luisa Potenza   M. Grudens Photo

People call and say the songs bring back treasured memories of growing up in their Italian homes where such music proliferated. It is not only pleasant memories that account for the staying power of these artists, but also an appreciation for voices that need no technical training.

Real talent, after all, is the ability to caress the ear and interpret a lyric as the lyricist meant them to be. The acknowledged master of this is Frank Sinatra. One cannot dispute the fact that Italian singers have always dominated the musical scene and continue to do so today.

For example, Filippo Voltaggio is a young composer and singer from California whose interpretation of popular songs sung in a soft, romantic voice, places him in the classic crooner category. His debut album, Reel Italian, is a compilation of songs from the cinema. His second, Love in Italiano, is a collection of ballads sung in Italian.

Filippo explained to me how and why he became a singer, and is featured here in a later chapter. Jerry Vale once said to me that he grew up in an environment of music, as did Al Martino, whom I caught up with at the Patchogue Theater last year when I hosted his benefit show, and Jimmy Roselli, where the emphasis was on Neapolitan classics introduced to Jimmy by his caretaker grandfather.

Crooning will never lose its appeal, despite the abundance of operatic tenors that are emerging on the scene. Like romance, this style of singing will never die.

So read on about the anecdotal stories of the Italian Crooners and how they achieved success, a must read for people who revere the inimitable style and showmanship of these artists.

Luisa Potenza
Host: Italia Mia
Every Sunday 11 AM - 1 PM
WALK 1370 AM - Long Island, New York

Illustration by James Sangiorgio

FRANKIE LAINE

"Mr. Rhythm"

Some Valid Views from Frankie Laine at 92 Years Young

Starting with the Big Bands in the 1930s, and continuing through today, we've been blessed with the opportunity to enjoy music that creates a feeling of well being and familiarity. Not the frenetic sounds of the various types of rock music, but the pure melodic sounds of some bands, their vocalists and the swinging jazz styles of others have provided a common bond between all people, no matter what their nationalities or social backgrounds.

Time, unfortunately, has robbed us of the pleasure of having most of the early "greats" among us physically, but their recordings survive them. One can't help but wonder how, for instance, Glenn Miller's style would have evolved over the years had he not met his untimely death. Or, how would Russ Columbo or Buddy Clark have fared over the years if their life was not cut short by an act of fate.

The Big Bands served a purpose aside from soothing our senses with their musical arrangements - they spawned such legendary singers as Doris Day, Kay Starr, and Frank Sinatra, to name a few. A follower of the great Al Jolson and Bing Crosby, as I was, Frank Sinatra spawned a number of Italian compatriots who really dug his phrasing and the way he interpreted the words to the music of his day.

I was one of those ethnic colleagues of Sinatra, as was Perry Como, Don Cornell, Jerry Vale, Tony Bennett, Jimmy Roselli, Dean Martin, Al Martino, Vic Damone, Julius La Rosa, Alan Dale, Bobby Darin, and even more.

These fine singers, with the exception of myself, Como and Cornell, out on their own without the benefit of an apprenticeship with a Big Band, did pretty good for a while. And, not to blow my own horn, I believe I was the first Italian male singer to achieve success sans a Big Band boost. For all of us it was definitely not an easy road, but I've never regretted any of the hardship, as I met many kind, helpful people on the way up. Among them were Perry Como, Carl Fischer, Al Jarvis, Hoagy Carmichael and Al Jolson. I'm sure the others had the same good fortune of people around them who propelled their own careers.

Today, there are still new singers coming up from every direction trying to make their way in this sometimes hard to penetrate business, especially since record companies are not sympathetic to the cause of "our kind of music." And, some of them are Italian, like Tony Babino-Tony B., John Primerano, Michael Bublé, Peter Cincotti, Tom Postilio, and still more, who are following in the great Italian tradition of always needing to sing, as we all needed to do before them.

Sinatra, and all of us, have set the stage for these young men to keep the music going. Only you can help them.

So, come read the anecdotes and facts about your favorite Italian singers as Richard Grudens unfolds the success stories about some of our best loved performers. They will always live in our hearts and, hopefully our children's, forever.

Frankie Laine
San Diego
August 26, 2004

Frankie
Laine

Wheels
Of A
Dream

BENEDETTO

Jacket Cover by Tony Bennett

Bel Canto

An Appreciation

Musicologist Theodore Grudzinski explains **Bel Canto.**

"An Italian phrase meaning 'Beautiful' is an expression that evolved from the 18th and 19th century Italian opera aria. The spectacular growth of the vocal virtuosity in Italy coupled with the tremendous range of emotional expression from the first operas of Monteverdi up to and beyond Donizetti, Bellini and Puccini produced an art form unrivaled in vocal agility, and packed with dramatic and emotional sensuality. *Bel Canto* became a powerful and popular musical style." Over the years the concept of *bel canto* spilled over into the provenance of popular song. The composers and the singers of popular music gradually evolved a crossover - a blend of what previously were two mutually exclusive styles of music. This was most evident in the recordings of ballads, sung and recorded by crooners such as Frank Sinatra, Perry Como and Bing Crosby. Many of these songs in *bel canto* style came out of the Broadway musical. 'Ol' Man River,' 'September Song,' 'Begin the Beguine,' 'You'll Never Walk Alone,' and 'Night and Day,' all sung and recorded by Sinatra. Of course, many other songs share the aesthetic of *bel canto.*

An Apology to The Great Italian Tenors

The subjects of this book are only Crooners, and unfortunately *not* Tenors.

Apologies to the world famous tenors.

We are unable to present the Italian tenor superstars that we all know, enjoy, and love. Among them, the great Mario Lanza, the charming Sergio Franchi, the king of them all, Enrico Caruso, the Italian smoothie,Carlo Buti, and the world famous Italian Tenors, the magnificent Placido Domingo and Luciano Pavarotti.

It would take a book of their own to properly showcase these wonderful Italian tenors.

The Author

The Great but Short Italian List of Songs with the Word Italy in the Title

"ALL OVER ITALY"

"THE ITALIAN STREET SONG"

"MAMBO ITALIANO"

"MARIE FROM SUNNY ITALY"

"ON THE SHORES OF ITALY"

"THERE'S A GARDEN IN OLD ITALY"

"WHEN IT'S NIGHT-TIME IN ITALY,

IT'S WEDNESDAY OVER HERE"

Torna A Surriento

COME BACK TO SORRENTO

Original song lyrics in Neapolitan with English Translation

by E. De Curtis and G.B. De Curtis

Vide 'O mare quant'e bello!

Spira tanta sentimento
Comme tu, a chi tiene mente,
Ca scetato, 'o faje sunna!'

Guarda qua' chisti ciardine,
Siente sie' 'sti sciure 'e arancio

Nu prufumo accussi fino,
Dint' 'o core se ne va

E tu dice: "Io parto, addio!"
T'alluntane da 'stu core,
Da la terra de ll 'ammore,
Tiene 'o core 'e nun turna'?!

Ma nun mme lassa',
Nun darme stu turmiento..
Torna a Surriento:
Famme campa'!

Vide 'o mare de Surriento
Chi tesore tene 'nfunno:
Chi ha girato tutt' 'o munno,
Nun ll'ha visto comm'a cca!

Guarda, attuorno, sti ssirene
Ca te guardano, 'ncantate
E te Vonno tantu bene:
Te vulessero vasa'!

E tu dice: "Io parto, addio!"
T'alluntane da 'stu core,
Da la terra de ll'ammore,
Tiene 'o core 'e nun turna'?!

Ma nun mme lassa',
Nun darme stu turmiento..
Torna a Surriento,
Femma campa'!

═══════════════════

**and in
English as Translated**

Look at the sea, it's so beautiful
It inspires such a strong feeling..
Just like you do to him who thinks of you,
You make him dream even awake.
Look, look at these gardens
Smell these orange blossoms
A scent so fine
It goes straight to your heart.

And you say, "I'm leaving, goodbye!"
You get far from this heart..
From the land of love,
Do you really not feel like coming back?

But don't leave me,
Don't give me such a pain..
Come back to Sorrento:
Let me live!

Look at the sea of Sorrento
Such treasures in its depths:
Even who traveled the whole world
Never saw the likes of this,

Look around, these mermaids
Look at you as if spellbound
They love you so much
They would like to kiss you!

And you say "I'm leaving, goodbye!"

Ervin Drake, Richard Grudens and Ben Grisafi (Photo Robert DeBetta)

Al Di La

by Ervin Drake and C. Donida
Original Italian words by Mogol

LOVE, the language of Italy has a phrase that embraces all of your graces:

Al Di La means that you are far above me, very far
Al Di La, as distant as the lovely evening star
Where you walk flowers bloom,
When you smile all the gloom turns into sunshine
And my heart opens wide
When you're gone it fades inside
And seems to have died;
Al Di La I wondered as I drifted where you were
Al Di La the fog around me lifted, there you were
In the kiss that I gave was the love I had saved for a lifetime
Then I knew all of you was completely mine!

Original Italian Lyrics

Al di la del bene piu prezioso, ci sei tu
Al di la del sogno piuambizio so, ci sei tu
Al di la delle cose piu belle al di la delle stelle, ci sei tu
Al di la ci sei tu per me, per me, soltanto per me
Al di la del mare piu profundo, ci sei tu
Al di la deilimiti del mondo, ci sei tu
Al di la della volta infinita al di la della vita, ci sei tu
Al di la ci sei tu, per me

The Great Ones

Francis Albert Sinatra

FRANK SINATRA: THE VOICE, SWOONATRA, SINATCH (coined by the Pied Pipers and Jo Stafford) THE INNKEEPER (a gracious host), NAPOLEON (by the Secret Service - CODE when with Presidential Events), THE CHAIRMAN OF THE BOARD (by disc Jockey WNEW, William B. Williams) and OL' BLUE EYES.

Dean Martin: "It's Frank Sinatra's world. We just live in it."

One of the Hoboken Four Goes Solo

What is there left to write about one of the greatest Italian crooners, Frank Sinatra? Frank's story was equally about his singing performances as well as his abstract and mecurial personality. In later years, unfortunately, Frank was mostly unavailable for interviews.

In 1997, for my book, *The Music Men*, his publicist **Susan Reynolds** reported:

> "As you may be aware, Mr. Sinatra is taking time off after more than 50 years performing concerts throughout the world. He appreciates your kind invitation to participate in your upcoming book *The Music Men,* but he is not taking on additional projects and is thus not available."

Frank was on a kind of health-hiatus at the time, and, realizing that no book about singers would be much of a success without his participation, we nevertheless proceeded without the benefit of a direct interview. Instead, we talked with a number of people who were able to provide a composite of worthwhile biographical material, thinking, that perhaps by gathering fresh comments and stories from those who knew and worked with him we may be able to contribute something special.

Almost everyone knows the Frank Sinatra story. Presented frequently on film and the subject of many books, authorized and unauthorized, Frank's turbulent life, private and public, has become open to all. His daughter, Nancy, has produced some remarkable and colorful coffee table books about her dad, positively presented, with endless, priceless photos.

My friend, once the best-known and best-loved disc jockey **William B. Williams,** long time host of the *Make Believe Ballroom* radio show on New York's WNEW, was a great friend to Frank Sinatra. It was William B. (as he was affectionately known) who coined the Sinatra sobriquet *Chairman of the Board,* which Frank, himself admitted he always tried to live up to. In 1984, Williams, who consistently said, "I don't care how a record sells, just how it sounds," held a rare interview with Frank on the air and sent me a copy of the tape which began:

"Hello World! This is William B. and I'd like to introduce you to Francis Albert Sinatra, a practically unknown singer. Say something, Francis, don't be shy!" (He chuckles.)

> "Hello World! This is Francis Albert Sinatra. You know, Willy B., about forty years ago I started at WNEW, and do you know what I got paid - zilch - but --they gave me thirty-five cents in carfare to get back to New Jersey. Well, I'm back again for those of you who ever wondered what happened to me. I know they're still paying the same kind of bread which may explain why Willy B. has been able to keep his job here."

Some time before that a guy named **Major Bowes** fronted a talent show on the radio called *The Amateur Hour,* a mini-version of today's *American Idol* television show, where performers got their start. One night in 1935, the Major introduced a new group:

"Good evening friends. We start the dizzy spin of the wheel of fortune...around and round she goes and where she stops nobody knows," the Major said in gravelly eloquence. "Now, first four youngsters in kinda nice suits - The Hoboken Four. They seem so happy, I guess, and they seem to make everybody else happy (gentle laughter from the audience). Tell me, where do you fellers work in Hoboken?"

"I'm Frank, Major. We're looking for jobs. How about it! (more appreciative laughter to Frank's good-natured boldness) Everyone that's ever heard us - liked us. We think we're pretty good."

"All right, what do you want to sing - or dance - or whatever it is you do?"

"We're gonna sing 'Shine' and then we're gonna dance." "All right! Let's have it!" Then the Major announced:" Here's the Hoboken Four." The boys closely and nicely emulated a Bing Crosby-Mills Brothers version of the then very popular song. They got the job. The Hoboken Four

Nancy and Frank

toured with the *Major Bowes Amateur Hour Show* earning seventy-five dollars a week.

"We were getting paid, so we were no longer amateurs," declared Frank, triumphantly.

It was a very slim looking Frank Sinatra in his first public appearance on the world's stages that would last over 62 musically eventful years. For most of those years he sang his heart out while the world listened.

Let's leap ahead some 10 years to 1945... things have changed. Frank was now singing to thousands of screaming bobby soxers at New York's Paramount Theater with the popular bands of Harry James, and later, Tommy Dorsey. Were you one of those screaming youngsters who helped catapult Frank to everlasting fame?

1n 1981, while interviewing Dorsey clarinetist **Johnny Mince**, he talked about meeting Sinatra for the first time:

"We were ready to go on a one-nighter, and Tommy says, 'C'mere, John.' He took me across the street and they had on a jukebox - playing that thing he did with Harry James - 'All or Nothing at All.' I said to Dorsey, 'Boy that guy is good!' But my impression when meeting Frank was something else. He was such a skinny, beat-up looking guy compared to Jack Leonard, our singer who just left the band, who had lots of class and was good-looking. Of course, Frank sure turned out to be the great one."

During my interview with **Harry James** in 1981, he said exactly this: "At that time Frank considered himself the greatest vocalist in the business. Get that! No one ever heard of him. He never had a hit record. He looked like a wet rag. But he tells me he's the greatest. He believed. And you know what, he was right."

By this time Frank was now out on his own as a single and

the screams and carrying on continued wherever he appeared. "Kiss me once and kiss me twice and kiss me once again....it's been a long, long time..." Frank's way of embracing a microphone with a new approach to putting over a song completely won over a fast growing female audience. He copied Bing Crosby and he absorbed Billie Holiday's way of bending a tune and coming back to center.

When he was with Harry James and Tommy Dorsey, Frank was the boy singer and **Connie Haines** was the girl singer: "I was just eighteen and I remember the police escorting Frank and me across the street from the Paramount over to the Astor Hotel, through the lobby into the drugstore just to get a hamburger," Connie and I have frequent conversations about the history of popular music of the time: "We could not get away from the screaming kids even to eat."

Connie Haines with Frank, 1939
(R. Grudens Collection)

Connie recalled some early enthusiasm three years before when they both sang with James. "Richard, it was something about the way he'd hang on to that microphone. Something in his singing that reached out to the audience - like he was saying... 'I'm giving this to you with everything I've got..what have you got to give me?' I guess they came backstage afterwards to tell him.

"Frank and I didn't always get along in those days, but, Frank showed his true colors one night - even though we were feuding while we sang the songs 'Let's Get Away from It All,' 'Oh, Look at Me Now,' and 'Snootie Little Cutie' -- when my dress caught fire because someone tossed a lit cigarette down from the balcony and it got snared in my dress netting. Tommy was still vamping, unaware of what was happening. Frank reacted quickly, throwing

23

his suit jacket over me and flinging me to the ground, snuffing out the flames - probably saving my life."

When Sinatra joined Tommy Dorsey, **Jo Stafford** was the lead singer of the Pied Pipers singing group: "Frank made a special effort to get a good blend with the Pipers. Most solo singers usually don't fit too well into a group, but Frank never stopped working at it and, of course, as you now know, he blended beautifully with us. He was meticulous about his phrasing and dynamics. He worked very hard so that his vibrato would match ours. And he was always conscientious about learning his parts. The first song I ever heard him sing was 'Stardust.' I thought, wow, this guy is destined for great success."

BING CROSBY: "FRANK IS A SINGER WHO COMES ALONG ONCE IN A LIFETIME, BUT WHY DID HE HAVE TO COME IN MY LIFETIME?"

In his book *Singers and the Song*, Gene Lees records Sinatra as the best singer he had ever heard and one of the best singers in history. "Sinatra learned breath control from Tommy Dorsey's technique of slowly and deliberately releasing air to support long lyrical melodic lines on his trombone and was indeed instructive to Sinatra. Dorsey would use this control to tie the end of one phrase into the start of the next. Sinatra learned to do the same."

Frank and Axel Stordahl (R. Grudens Collection)

Tony Bennett first heard Frank Sinatra sing at the Paramount. "I bought my date a gardenia and took her to the Paramount. It was a beautiful show and his repertoire was all quality music. I was very impressed. He had a fantastic consistency as a performer which has always encouraged my own singing career. He had a magic voice."

FRANK SINATRA TALKS ABOUT LEARNING PHRASING FROM TOMMY DORSEY'S TROMBONE PLAYING

"I used to sit behind him on the bandstand and watch, trying to see him sneak a breath. But I never saw the bellows move in his back. His jacket didn't even move. So I edged my chair around to the side a little and peeked around to watch him. Finally, I discovered he had a 'sneak pinhole' in the corner of his mouth---not an actual hole but a tiny place he left open where he was breathing. In the middle of a phrase, while the tone was still being carried through the trombone, he'd go 'shhh' and take a quick breath and play another four bars. So I began to 'play' my voice like he did with his trombone."

Sinatra's first recordings with Columbia Records exposed the public to a former band singer who no longer sang songs to which you could only dance. Axel Stordahl was his arranger, helped too, by arranger George Siravo. Frank was just twenty-six and Stordahl about the same. Both Dorsey alumni, they produced some classic sides together with music that had some imagination and gutty arrangements. Remember "Dream," "The Girl That I Marry," "Put Your Dreams Away," and "Day by Day?"

At the end of the 1940s, Frank Sinatra's career changed. He rebelled against Columbia's chief Mitch Miller, who was producing his own kind of music, that bothered Sinatra, and which he thought demeaned his skills as a singer. He would not sing those silly ditties Miller had set for him to record.

Talking with **Rosemary Clooney** in 1986, she loved Frank. Manie Sacks, A & R man at Columbia and later one of my own friends at NBC, answered Sinatra's request for a girl singer by suggesting Rosemary. Frank said O.K.

"We did two sides of that first date together, but later on we did some other things. That first session was the thrill of my life because I was such a fan. I adored him when I was in high school, and it was great working with him. He kept up the quality in every recording date."

By 1952, Frank Sinatra was without a movie or recording contract, or even management. Because of those late 1940s forty-five to fifty shows a week, which meant 100 songs a day, the great voice tired, his personal life tumbling into a shambles. But, Frank Sinatra promptly restarted on the road to an even greater success than he had known before, propelled by his acting only role in the film *From Here to Eternity,* his move from Columbia to Johnny Mercer's Capitol Records, and his union with master arranger Nelson Riddle.

(Courtesy CBS)

Nelson taught Frank how to swing. Their first album was, what else, *Swing Easy,* followed by *Songs for Young Lovers* (Nelson with Siravo), and In the *Wee Small Hours of the Morning,* literally revising his recording career. He proceeded to record over twenty albums from 1953 to 1961, all hits. Some of the songs: "Just One of Those Things," "My Funny Valentine," "A Foggy Day," "Last Night When Were Young," "This Love of Mine," (he co-wrote this one earlier) and "What is This Thing Called Love?"

> *"Sinatra shocks. Sinatra jolts. Sinatra arouses our anger and our passion by expressing his own. Sinatra gets our pulses to race and our brain to click."* Will Friedwald-from his book *Jazz Singing.*

"I first met Frank Sinatra when we was with Tommy Dorsey," said **Duke Ellington** in 1973, "They all came down one night at

At the Paramount - (R. Grudens Collection)

the College Inn at the Sherman Hotel in Chicago where we were playing, about the time he was ready to split the Dorsey gig. I could tell that by the way Tommy said *good night* to him. He was young, crispy-crunch fresh, and the girls were squealing then. He was easy to get along with, and there were no hassles about his music. Every song he sings is understandable and, most of all, believable, which is the ultimate in theater. And I must repeat and emphasize my admiration for him as a nonconformist. When he played the Paramount the chicks were screaming. He was an individualist, nobody tells him what to do."

In the late 1960s, both Sinatra and Ellington were playing Las Vegas, and Frank was having a birthday party. Ellington asked permission from the management to go over and play a few numbers for Frank. They did and they had a ball. "I thanked Frank for the great time and told him it was the best party he ever gave for Paul Gonsalves (Ellington sideman), who had such a great time he had to be carried out bodily."

"In 1961, my father asked Morris "Mo" Ostin, who was with Verve Records, to head up his own label, "Reprise," said daughter, Nancy," It was very important for dad to have his own recording company."

According to Frank himself, "I always like to choose my own songs for an album...to keep all the songs in the same genre' - swing, love songs, etcetera. Once I decide what type of music I want, I make up a list of song titles, and my associates - arrangers - suggest songs. When we actually get down to where arrangements have to be done, I go through the list again and pick out eight to ten songs and go with them." The first Reprise selections were "A Foggy Day," "A Fine Romance," and "Be Careful, It's My Heart."

When I talked with legendary jazz vibraphonist **Red Norvo** in 1998, he championed Frank as a *great* singer: "We worked together in Vegas and then at the Fountainbleu in Florida and also in Atlantic City. We also went on tour in Australia. I was used to handling singers in my various bands (Red Norvo was married to the first regular big band singer Mildred Bailey and is a recognized Jazz Master,) so Frank was never a problem to me. When we first worked together, I had a trio, which was too small, so I told him we needed a drummer and sax, and he said OK. We made a couple of movies - *Kings Go Forth,* where I wrote some of the music, and *Oceans Eleven,* a kinda funny movie where Frank plays a bank robber in Vegas. Our Capitol recordings of the late sixties are just being issued now. Heard they are number four on the charts. Isn't that somethin'?"

Frank Sinatra continued his singing activities, although he really did not do many Italian numbers as some of his counterparts were singing. He announced his retirement in 1971, after pouring out albums like *Cycles, A Man Alone,* and the closer *My Way,* in the late sixties. He returned gradually doing some concerts into 1973 and producing an album, *Ol' Blue Eyes Is Back,* arranged by Gordon Jenkins and Don Costa. The songs: "Send in the Clowns," and "You Will Be My Music."

Frank toured triumphantly with Woody Herman in 1974 and spawned the album *The Main Event.* The songs: "The Lady is a Tramp," "I Get a Kick Out of You," "Autumn in New York," "My Kind of Town," and "My Way."

1975 produced a series of appearances at the Uris Theater in New York and then London with the driving band of Count Basie which included the presence of the *divine* Sarah Vaughan.
In the eighties, Quincy Jones' talents became linked to Sinatra's musical career, beginning with the album *L.A. Is My Lady.*
"Frank is remarkable. When we recorded at A & M studios in New York, I called the orchestra for three hours before. We rehearsed and set the balance. Frank came in at seven o'clock and, so help me God, at eight-twenty he went home. We had done three songs, "he said. The songs: "Stormy Weather," "How Do You Keep the Music Playing?" and "After You've Gone."

In his book, *Sinatra-An American Classic,* John Rockwell, "The basic technique is Italian, the flexible flow of classic *bel canto*; so is the penchant for heartfelt melodiousness." He also considers Sinatra's album *Only the Lonely* his best: "...deeply emotional songs, telling arrangements and interpretive maturity," and further, "He remains a vital contributor to the Tin Pan Alley tradition that nurtured him, and that he, in turn, has done so much, for so long, to sustain."

My favorite Sinatra recording is an early swinging gem, "Sweet Lorraine," a perfect blend of voice and instrument. It features jazz all-stars with Nat "King" Cole on piano, Johnny Hodges on alto sax, Charlie Shavers on trumpet, Coleman Hawkins on tenor sax, and Eddie Safranski (one of my old NBC buddies) on bass. Amazing group. Amazing music. Find it. You'll love it.

Frank Sinatra appeared in many films, but did not sing in all of them. We'll leave that material for film writers to ponder.

Once, appearing with William B. at WNEW on the Make Believe Ballroom, Frank had a speaking part: "Hi there, my name is Francis Albert Sinatra and I've got news for you. Here is your host William B. Williams."

Richard Grudens and William B. Williams
(Camille Smith Photo)

"Name dropper!" William B. answered tongue-in-cheek, "A question, Francis, that is somewhat philosophic. I know how keenly you feel about your family and your two granddaughters. The legacy that you leave them, is there any particular way you want to be remembered as a man...as a performer...as an American...as a human being?"

"Well, Willy, I realize it's a broad question, but I can narrow it by saying that I'd like to be remembered as a man who was as honest as he knew how to be in his life and as honest as he knew how to be in his work...and a man who gave as much energy in what he did every day as anybody else ever did. I'd like to be remembered as a decent father, as a fair husband, and as a great granddad...wonderful grandpop. And, I'd like to be remembered as a good friend to my friends."

William B.: "I think the only addendum he would have added is ...as a man who *enjoyed*."

Frank and Barbara Sinatra (Courtesy B. Sinatra)

Frank: "Ah! That's true. I didn't want to get into that because, you know, there's an old 14th century Spanish adage... 'living well is the best revenge'...If that applied to anybody, it must apply to me." Frank was also being philosophical.

"I knew many men like that in my lifetime," He continued, "a guy name Errol Flynn...John Barrymore, even (Humphrey) Bogart. All those great men who are now gone-they came to play. That lifestyle is almost gone now. People like Rubirosa and other men I met around New York through the years. People like Toots Shor - it's nearly gone now. I assume I may be one of the last of that kind. I think that's what we're here for...to make the best of every day, to get the most out of every day...and I worked like Hell to do that, too!"

Frank Sinatra has always worked for the benefit of those in need. Helen O'Connell told me that Frank secretly paid all the medical bills for fellow singer Bob Eberly. Frank always contributed his time and talent for the Italian American Organization through personal appearances to raise needed funds.

William B. also once told me about Frank's great work that gathered millions for Sloan-Kettering Memorial Cancer Hospital in New York. At the 67th Street outpatient entrance between York and Ist Avenue of that hospital there is a plaque on the wall that states:"

> # "This Wing of Sloan-Kettering is
> # Through the Efforts of Frank Sinatra"

During his final years, Frank and Barbara Sinatra worked hard for the Barbara Sinatra Children's Center at Eisenhower Center, Rancho Mirage, California. And, profits from their book, *The Sinatra Celebrity Cookbook,* by Barbara Frank & Friends, have supported that worthy project.

Finally, my friend **Jerry Vale** had this to say about his friend:

"There were great times with Frank and his friends, like our many card games on Sunday afternoon at four o'clock. Angie Dickinson, Jack Lemmon and his wife, Felicia, Gregory Peck, and M*A*S*H comedy writer Larry Gelbart, and others, would really have a lot of fun telling jokes and recounting stories about the old days - good and bad - when we were all young and coming up. Later, when we would play cards and Frank was preoccupied with his illness, he would say, "Hey, you guys, finish the game, I'm going to bed - I'm tired." I objected, saying 'C'mon Frank, stay up and finish the game. You're bringing me luck. Don't you remember singing 'Luck Be a Lady?' Don't sleep now, they'll be plenty of time for that all week."

Jerry was trying to keep Frank in the game. He didn't want him to give in. As time went by, Frank became worse and suspended those legendary Sunday get togethers. Jerry would visit his home anyway as he did a hundred times before. Barbara would receive him warmly, then excuse herself to bring her husband out to greet him.

"Hello, Jerry."

Jerry turned to see Frank standing there and could not avoid the feeling of emotional attachment.

"I was very upset seeing my teacher, my friend, Frank Sinatra, in that condition, his health deteriorated. It hurt, but wear and tear, illness and age had taken its toll. I guess it happens to everyone sooner or later."

The world lost the distinguished voice of Frank Sinatra in 1998.

Frank with Nancy Sr.

Frank with Actor Alan Ladd

Sledding with Little Nancy

On NYC Radio WNYC

That's Life

D. Kay and K. Gordon

That's life,
That's what all the people say.
You're riding high in April,
Shot down in May.
But I know I'm gonna change my tune
When I'm back on top in June

I said, that's life
Funny as it seems
Some people get their kicks
Steppin' on a dream
But I, I don't let it get me down
'Cause this ol' world keeps spinnin' round

I've been a puppet, a pauper, a pirate, a poet, a pawn and a king.
I've been up and down and over and out and
I know one thing:
Each time I find myself flat on my face
I pick myself up and get back in the race.

That's life.
I can't deny it.
I thought of quitting, babe,
But my heart won't buy it.
If I didn't think it was worth a quick try
I'd just roll myself up in a big ball and die.

Sinatra Music

Author's Choice:

I believe the Best Sinatra album is *The Columbia Years*, a 12 CD collection comprising everything he recorded at Columbia between 1943 and 1952 that includes the masterpieces of the period "If You Are But a Dream," "Nancy with the Laughing Face," "Embraceable You," "She's Funny That Way," "Melancholy Baby," "Dream," "I Don't Know Why," "A Ghost of a Chance," "How Deep is the Ocean," "The Things We did Last Summer," "Time After Time," "Always," "I Concentrate on You," "Laura," "Spring is Here," "Fools Rush In," "I'm Glad There is You," "Autumn in New York," "Night and Day," and "I'm a Fool to Want You." Every one a classic winner.

Frank's Capitol albums with Nelson Riddle consists of expressions of emotions at an extended length at a time when technology introduced the long playing record and high fidelity. *In the Wee Small Hours of the Morning, Only the Lonely, Songs for Swingin' Lovers* and *A Swinging Affair* were the best and the first

of the Capitol-Sinatra-Riddle collaboration. *Only the Lonely* remained on the charts for one hundred and twenty weeks, and later, *Come Dance with Me* stayed on the charts for a hundred and forty weeks.

Frank at Capitol Records

Sinatra Impressions

In 1992, while attending a creative writing class, a young man named **Mathew Pacciano** was handed an assignment to write a snippet about a popular figure and not mention the name, yet compose it so a reader can readily identify the subject. He chose to write about Frank Sinatra whom he witnessed performing at a Sloan Kettering Benefit in New York City.

Ol' Blue Eyes

The smoke in the room, a bluish veil clinging to the ceiling, was as much a part of the setting and the staging as was the microphone and stool he would sit upon. The clinking of a sea of glasses and subdued chatter of voices, coupled with the movement of the waiters, placed a final touch to the mood.

Soon he would appear to make his usual entrance: sauntering across the stage, cigarette in hand, so sure, almost cocky, as he reached for the stool and microphone. The orchestra was waiting: tuned, poised, ready.

The house was full. People were dressed to the hilt, some with diamonds reflecting their flickers of light as women moved about. The waiters carefully moved to the rear. There was a hush, followed by an eerie silence, and then darkness. The spotlight cut a path through the smoke, and a hidden voice, quietly at first, then suddenly booming, announced his name. The crowd quickly came to life.

The orchestra played his familiar theme and there he was moving ahead gracefully into the center of a gigantic ball of light. He bowed and thanked his audience for the thunderous applause and began. He belted out song after song, holding his head at a provocative tilt as he reached certain notes. Then, looking up, then down, arms close to body, then outstretched, his intense blue eyes always reached out to someone.

His voice, never overpowering, although sometimes strained when demands required. It was a voice of character and experience. His diction was flawless, his phrasing and timing masterful. He was a craftsman, putting together a powerful performance with a believable voice with a host of meticulous details.

The applause, the smiles, the tears, told why they were there. Each song touched someone. Some brought back memories of youth, or of carefree days gone by. Others reminisced - perhaps broken hearts, shattered romances, and the 'why didn't this ever happen to me look' appeared on many faces. For the few young people present, he created a temporary mystique.

The man, middle aged. The songs, dug up from archives. The voice, legendary perfect. A dynamic personality with unbounded charm and charisma held them all in awe for almost two hours. When he made his final bow, he seemed humble. And when he looked up and smiled broadly - his blue eyes actually twinkled. You knew who he was. And so did he.

Sinatra Sauce

Although Frank Sinatra employed a chef, he was known for puttering around the kitchen cooking up spaghetti sauce in the morning hours. Here is his favorite veal dish.

Veal Piccata

The ingredients:
1/8 lb butter
1/4 lb margarine
juice of one lemon
capers
8 veal strips, each one inch wide and 1/4" thick, flattened to 1/8".
1 egg beaten slightly
Salt and Pepper to taste
4 slices eggplant, peeled to 1/2" thick
Bread Crumbs
1/4 lb additional butter.

Directions: Melt 1/8 lb butter in a skillet. Add lemon, capers and veal. Saute veal 1-1/2 to 2 minutes, until lightly brown and firm to the touch. Remove to warm serving platter and place in oven on low heat.

Combine egg, salt and pepper in a bowl. Dip eggplant slices in egg batter and cover with bread crumbs. Heat 1/4 lb butter or margarine in skillet. Add eggplant and toss with wooden spoon over high heat for about 5 minutes or until tender and beginning to brown.

Remove the veal from the oven. Serve veal on top of eggplant slices. Garnish with lemon wedges, parsley or mint, if desired.

Louis Prima

The Great Entertainer - Italian Musical Hero - Too Often Overlooked

Solid, Jack!

Crazy, man!

I have always associated Louis Prima with bouncy, staccato jazz singing, delivering that truly original Italian "Godfather style" throaty voicing on favorites like "Angelina," (his mom's name) "Just a Gigolo," "Civilization," and "That Old Black Magic," performed with comedy antics, while fronting his own band in New York theaters and night clubs during the 1930s through the 1970s. Aside from that prolific talent, few realize that Louis (pronounced *Louie*) was the composer of the great jazz anthem "Sing, Sing, Sing" the jazz explosion composition that rocked Carnegie Hall when Benny Goodman, Harry James, Gene Krupa, and Count Basie performed it *live* back in 1938 during the very first jazz concert performed in that hallowed hall. The song was originally intended for Bing Crosby and named "Sing, Bing, Sing." Louis and Bing were friends and co-performers and shared a love for horse racing, Louis appearing in Bing's 1936 film *Rhythm On the Range.*

Born in New Orleans of Sicilian parents on December 7, 1910, Louis soaked up the music of the city he would always love, a city full of a mixture of many jazz cultures. First a violin player, then, inspired by local jazz musicians, a quality trumpeter, he eventually rose to became a main attraction on New York's famed 52nd Street, later renamed "Swing Street" in his well-earned honor. By the late 1920s, Louis had started a few musical groups, then moved to Cleveland, then to Chicago, and finally in the 1930s, to New York City, performing as Louis Prima & His New Orleans Gang. Five years later, in February of 1935, he became the sensational first opening act at the *Famous Door* on 52nd Street billed as the New Orleans Five and turned that venue into the hottest club in town. His showmanship soon began drawing crowds of faithful fans who became as interested in his comedy as his fine jazz musicianship.

What a good year for jazz musicians with Basie at Loew's State, Tommy Dorsey at the Commodore Hotel, Casa Loma at the New Yorker, Chick Webb at the Savoy, Cab Calloway at the Cotton Club, and Louis Prima and pianist Art Tatum at the Famous Door.

"Prima and his perpetrators of merry mayhem are the nearest thing to perpetual motion in show business. This act is so fresh, it looks as if he is making it up as he goes along." Gene Knight, *New York Journal American.*

"I got lucky early," Louis would often say, "and I let the crowd know I was solid Italian and from New Orleans."

Throughout the 1940s, Louis continued to be a sensation with his jivy singing and Sicilian slang and some very fractured, but lovable English material. Of all the great New Orleans trumpet players, like Louis Armstrong, Louis delivered his personal and exclusive comedy, breaking up an audience, which, by now, had become endeared to him. He brought fun onto the dance floor with his wild antics.

As George Simon noted in his book The Big Bands:

"Prima's success is both a healthy and a happy phenomenon. Louis just goes out there and has a helluva good time, acting like a natural showman, kidding around, poking fun at folks out front, at guys in his band, and, most of all, at himself."

It is interesting to realize that in the early years Louis Prima became the first entertainer, as both bandleader and vocalist, to introduce and record Italian songs to the American public. As everyone knows, Louis was an accomplished, first-class musician with a feeling for jazz, better than most trumpeters of his day. He knew how to run and manage a band, and, like Glenn

Miller, how to be commercially successful. Many noted sidemen appeared with him over the years; Pee Wee Russell, Nappy Lamare, Claude Thornhill, George Van Epps, and Ray Boudac. Louis collaborated on the million selling Claude Thornhill/Fran Warren recording "Sunday Kind of Love."

Louis appeared in a number of films, including, *Rhythm On the Range, Manhattan Merry-Go-Round, Start Cheering,* and *You Can't Have Everything.*

Sam Butera joined him in the 1950s and became the band's featured sax player. Gradually moving on to Las Vegas venues, Louis performed his previously popular "I Ain't Got Nobody" (more fractured

Louis with Sam Butera (Gia Prima Collection)

English) and "Just a Gigolo" exuberant medley scoring well in the hot spots with his then new wife, vocalist Keely Smith, with Sam Butera and The Witnesses.

"Vegas was the best spot in the early years," Louis said, "but then it got too big and you got lost with all the other acts. But I ran my act regularly at the Sands, the Sahara, the Desert Inn, and the Hilton."

Louis Prima capped his memorable and terrific career performing a voice-over in a 1967 Walt Disney film *Jungle Book* playing the part of *King Louie,* an orangutan, singing "I Wanna Be Like You." He was very proud of participating in that movie, that brought him even wider fame.

Louis' act was sometimes so wild, the audience didn't always know what to expect. A great musician and very talented musical comedian, Louis' final performances were to be at the Tropicana in 1975.

Lately, in Las Vegas, Louis' daughter, Lena Prima, is

performing a tribute show to her dad, headlining it "Louis Prima: That's My Dad."

Her song list includes songs that her dad made famous, "Sing, Sing, Sing," "Buona Sera," "Angelina," "Oh! Marie," "When You're Smiling," and "Che la Luna," among others. She *jumps, jives and wails* and absolutely pleases her audience. This is not just a nostalgic act, her dramatic performance of "Mama" is really something special. Lena also does a great rendition of "Mambo Italiano," an early Rosemary Clooney hit.

Lena's mom, of course, is Gia Maione Prima, whom Louis discovered one day in 1962 working at a Howard Johnson's in Toms River, New Jersey. This, not long after his split with band vocalist Keely Smith, whom Louis had to replace. Although Gia was trained in classical voice, she possesses that same husky timbre that complimented Louis' own unique singing sound. After an audition at the Latin Casino, arranged by her uncle who owned a night club in New Jersey, and knew Rolly Dee who worked with Louis, she handily landed the job as the band's new vocalist. Louis thought she was just perfect for the job. "That was on Mother's Day in 1962. As fate would have it, Louis and I were married a year later." said Gia, "It was meant to be."

She first performed with Louis at New York's Basin Street where she totally captured the hearts of the press and her audience who included Peggy Lee, Ella Fitzgerald, and Jackie Gleason, all who sat up front and enthusiastically cheered her on. Some thought Louis would not fare well without Keely Smith, but Gia proved otherwise. Gia did not try to emulate Keely's deadpan style, instead she developed her own act receiving help and encouragement from Louis and Sam Butera and the other musicians.

"A Star is born. Her name is Gia Maione, she's young, slim and very pretty. Two weeks ago she was a waitress in Howard Johnson's; yesterday afternoon she was coiffed and dressed in a new and different manner. Last midnight, she wowed her audience with her performance and was cheered for two whole minutes after she left the Basin Street stage for the very first time in her young life."

Nick Lapole, music critic, October 13, 1962.

Speaking recently to Gia Prima at her home on the New Jersey shore, not far from a favorite Louis Prima venue, Atlantic City, we talked about her career with Louis and just how happy her days were with her amazing husband.

Louis and Gia with Frank Sinatra (Gia Prima Collection)

Never intimidated by Louis Prima's fame when she first joined the band, unknown to him, Gia had grown to admire him from afar. Her dad was a Prima fan and Gia heard and had enjoyed his recordings from her earliest recollection:

"After my dad took me to see *his* idol Louis Prima in a live performance when I was just a little kid, I became attached to Louis Prima in every way. When I was fourteen, I met him face to face and secured a coveted prize - his autograph, which I have always cherished. When I won that audition, I realized I would be working with my one and only idol, ever. It was, for me, a Cinderella story come true.

"When I finally got to work with Louis, I don't know where

idolatry ended and love began. I was always so comfortable with the aura of Louis, so when I joined the band it was easy for me to "fit in" being totally familiar with every chart through my precious Louis Prima record collection. It was as though I had known him all my life-and, in a way, I guess I had."

When Gia is on stage she is always comfortable, always feeling the barrier of protection the stage offers: "In that way it's different than with one on one relationships, otherwise I am generally shy with people."

When Louis and Gia decided to marry, it happened exactly this way: "Louis never really proposed. One day, however, in-between shows at Harrah's in Lake Tahoe, Louis asked me to meet him at the side entrance. Puzzled, I found him there waiting in a limo with both his friends, Rolly Dee and Pat Francellini. I thought perhaps he didn't like my performances and was escorting me to the airport

Louis, Gia, Louis, Jr. and Lena (Gia Prima Collection)

to send me home. But, upon entering the limo, he breathlessly presented me with two beautiful rings and we promptly drove to close-by Minden, Nevada, and were married by a justice of the peace. It was so romantic. Rolly Dee was best man and Pat, a witness. After the ceremony we drove back and finished the third show. After the show, Louis led me to a room prepared as a surprise for our private wedding reception with a most beautiful wedding cake. At the next show Louis introduced me as *Mrs. Prima*, to the surprise of everyone."

Gia's parents were concerned about the difference in age between fifty-two year old Louis and twenty-one year old Gia, but she reassured them citing Louis' ageless drive, youthful stamina, and sterling disposition, setting him apart from other possible suitors. Anyway, she had loved him for her entire life in fantasy and now it was a treasured reality. The age problem would make no difference. She loved him, and he, her. That's all she needed. "Our life together was simply wonderful, Richard. Louis was always so caring, molding me, teaching me, and we never had a cross word between us, ever. He idolized the children. He was to them a playful Teddy bear."

Gia and Louis Prima worked successfully together up through 1975 when Louis became ill following a brain operation and lapsed into a coma in which state he remained for three years, Gia always at his bedside. Louis passed on in 1978, leaving Gia, Louis, Jr. and Lena to carry on his legacy. Gia is now sixty-three years young, and carefully maintains and manages the legacy and business of her husband with help from her good friend Ron Cannatella, author and broadcaster.

Lena Prima

I talked with Lena Prima and discovered her enthusiasm for presenting her dad's works to some old, and some new fans in Las Vegas and everywhere else she appears:

"I was working with a small band called Spiral Staircase, and we were aboard a cruise ship, where I just did a few songs that my mom and dad did - a little fifteen minute thing - I talked about my dad and the people responded wildly and lined up after each show and told me stories and how much his music meant to them. They would skip school to go to see him. They thought I should put on a whole show based on his music.

"My co-performers urged me on as well. I did it because it makes all those people happy. They light up and are reliving memories. My dad was one of those one-of-a-kind guys."

Of course, Lena loves the music that seems to be imbedded in her soul. From Chicago to Miami, New Jersey to Las Vegas, Lena is on a personal quest, encouraged by everyone she meets - especially when they realize who she is and what she is accomplishing.

Lena Prima

"I do about a ninety minute show, and slip in one of my own, a ditty called "Silly in the Middle." It's an upbeat, swing number that really goes over. My brother, Louis, comes in on the weekend and he does a couple of tribute songs, too."

It was hard for Lena to select her favorite Louis Prima song to perform: "Because, I love all of them," she said. Lena feels grateful to be working and will keep going until the people stop coming to see her, which may be a very long time. Lena is vivacious and simply a self-described singer, "That's what I do and will keep doing." I detected a natural enthusiasm in her voice. I guess it runs in the family.

GIA'S LIST OF LOUIS PRIMA'S
BEST MUSICAL PERFORMANCES

1. BUONA SERA
2. ANGELINA
3. OH, MARIE
4. CHE LA LUNA
5. JUST A GIGOLO-I AIN'T GOT NOBODY
6. JUMP, JIVE & WAIL
7. BASIN STREET-SLEEPY TIME DOWN SOUTH
8. CIVILIZATION
9. ROBIN HOOD
10. THAT OLD BLACK MAGIC

Sam Butera He's from Sicily, too!

Sam Butera began his musical career very early too, just as Louis did, but with a saxophone. And, he was born in New Orleans too, like Louis, but a bit later - in 1926. In a contest held at famed Carnegie Hall in New York, in 1946, Sam was hailed the *Outstanding Teenage Musician in America* by Look Magazine. He was nineteen.

Later Sam played in Ray McKinley's band and in the bands of Tommy Dorsey and Al Hirt. "I learned a lot about phrasing with other guys when I was with those bands. But, I didn't stay long."

When Louis was searching for an all around, premium sax player, Louis' brother Leon recommended Sam, who, at once, joined Louis and Keely Smith and performed their Las Vegas act as the featured player, performing with Louis what was coined the Shuffle Beat. Together they recorded several albums and

Sam Butera and Ron Canatella
(R. Canatella Collection)

49

performed on dozens of TV shows and several movies.

Sam recorded on his own on Cadence and Capitol Records. Alone and with the Louis Prima band, Sam has appeared with Frank Sinatra nationally and with Jerry Vale, Sergio Franchi, Jimmy Roselli, and Sammy Davis. For all his efforts in Las Vegas venues, Sam received both the *Lifetime Achievement* and *Entertainer of the Year* Awards by the revered *Augustus Society*.

Today, Sam Butera is officially retired, but his group, *The Wildest* performs regularly, appearing recently with Al Martino at the Westbury Music Fair on Long Island.

THE 1962 WITNESSES: SAM BUTERA vocals and tenor sax; Bobby Seltzer - vocal and guitar; Lou Sino - trombone; John Nagy - piano; Jimmy Vincent- drums; Rolly Dee - vocal, string bass, and Morgan Thomas, clarinet, alto sax, valve trombone, and flute.

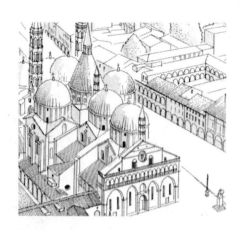

Louis Prima Recipe

Here is one of Louis Prima's favorite recipes sent to me
recently by Gia Prima with pride.

LINGUINE WITH CLAM SAUCE

(6) 6-1/2 oz. cans minced clams
4 large cloves finely chopped garlic
1/3 cup dry white wine (not sweet)
1/2 tbs. Mediterranean oregano
Crushed red pepper (to taste)
1/3 cup Bertolli olive oil

Have all ingredients ready. Bring pot of salted water to a boil.
Add pasta. While that is cooking, add first 7 ingredients to a deep
fry pan. Bring to a heavy simmer, then reduce heat. By this time the
pasta should be almost cooked. When done, strain WELL. Place in
bowls, then top with your
clam sauce. Serve with
your grated romano and
some really good Italian
bread, wine and perhaps
a nice salad.

PRETEND YOU DON'T SEE HER

Words and Music by **STEVE ALLEN**

RECORDED BY
JERRY VALE
ON CORONET

CHAPPELL & CO. LTD.
(Incorporated in Great Britain)
NATIONAL BLDG., 250 PITT ST., SYDNEY
and 10 Willis Street, Wellington, NEW ZEALAND
BREGMAN, VOCCO & CONN LTD., 50 New Bond St., London
BREGMAN, VOCCO & CONN INC., NEW YORK

Authorised for sale only in
Australia and New Zealand

2/6

3

(Courtesy Jerry Vale)

Genaro Louis Vitaliano

Jerry Vale - The Silver Fox

In 1998, after completing *The Music Men*, my book showcasing the men singers of the Golden Age of Music, I received a letter from a man in England who had purchased the book: "Do you know if there is a book written about Jerry Vale's life? If there is, please send me a copy or tell me where I may buy one."

Well, Jerry was one of the subjects in *The Music Men* so I forwarded the request on to him in Los Angeles, adding, "If you don't have one, call me and we'll write one." He didn't so we wrote one. We entitled it *Jerry Vale-A Singer's life.* You can buy a copy on www.richardgrudens.com or at your favorite book store.

Jerry and Conductor Glenn Osser at Columbia

As attested to by an enviable number of fellow show business admirers, Jerry Vale is clearly one of the good guys in the business whom everybody loves. Jerry and I originally got together in the fall of 1997, and have been friends ever since. We traveled together for a couple of years working through a number of book signings at restaurants and theaters and appeared in radio and television interviews here and there and got to know one another quite well.

Jerry Vale's great musical hero was the one and only Perry Como:

"I always wanted to become a singer after listening to him and Frank Sinatra on my 78 RPM phonograph back in my room in the Bronx where I grew up. I tried to sing along while playing their recordings. That's how I learned. "Jerry's first experience came one night at a local Bronx night spot called Club Del Rio when the MC called out during the windup of a singing contest, Anybody else want to try out singing tonight?"

(Courtesy Columbia/Sony)

Knowing Jerry was kind of reserved about singing publicly, a friend literally pushed him out onto the stage and called out, "Here he is! *Jerry Como.*" Jerry performed the haunting "Far Away Places" and easily won the contest.

"When I heard the applause, I knew I would become a professional singer one day." He still hears the applause. Jerry went on to perform at the Stardust Ballroom in the Bronx with a fourteen piece band. He began crooning mostly love songs and still sings love songs today:

"I like to sing songs that tell a story, have a pretty melody, nice lyrics, and that are sentimental. It was always my choice to perform that kind of material," which he has proved to everyone over the years within his over 50 albums for Columbia Records. He loves singing Italian songs like "Non Dimenticar," "Arriverderci

Roma," "Come Back to Sorrento," "Anema e Core," and "Ciao Ciao Bambina." Favorites like "Pretend You Don't See Her," or "Al Di La," our mutual friend Ervin Drake's great Italian tune, is another popular request when Jerry performs.

"Much of my music is like a romantic trip to Italy. They are such rich gems, which is why I choose to sing them. My faithful fans count on that."

Richard, Jerry and Rita at Borders, Farmingdale, L.I. - 2002 (Jerry Castleman Photo)

It was singer Guy Mitchell who first brought Jerry to Columbia A & R man Mitch Miller after singing with him on the same bill: "I could not believe it. Here was a guy who opened for me on the same billing who sang better than I did," Guy once told me.

At the time, Miller was guiding the early careers of Tony Bennett, Rosemary Clooney, Guy Mitchell, Johnny Ray, and Frankie Laine.

Jerry's first recording for Columbia under Mitchell was his own favorite "Two Purple Shadows," and his most requested song at concerts. Up to a year or so ago, Jerry played the Florida circuit for the *Fiesta Italiano*, where many of you have seen him perform with fellow singers Julius La Rosa, Don Cornell, Anna Maria Alberghetti, and earlier, Frankie Laine.

Jerry has been happily married to dancer and actress Rita Grable for 46 years. They have a son, Robert, and a daughter, Pamela, mother of a now spoiled grandson, Logan.

As his late friend Buddy Hackett, who wrote the foreword for Jerry's book, said "Anybody can have a friendship that lasts more than forty years. The trick is to live long enough. The other components are trust, caring, crying (when necessary), and above all, laughter, which is vital to a forty-year relationship. My family, and Jerry Vale and his beautiful wife and family, had those components. Jerry never left an audience unsatisfied or ever deserted a friend in need."

From June 1999 on, there was no letup as Jerry and I worked and reworked the manuscript of Jerry's book into a viable, valid biography of his life in music. With Jerry, it was the stories, the backstage portraits, the big break, the heartbreak, the heights and

Jerry and Richard at WALK Radio (B. Grisafi Photo)

Vic Damone, Sammy Davis, Jerry Vale and Jack Jones (J. Vale Collection)

depths of his career, the never-ending hard work, and all the complexities that comprise a life in show business, dramatized and placed perceptively into print.

When Jerry would perform at Long Island's Westbury Music Fair, he would announce the presence of the book being offered for sale in the lobby after the show: "If you stop buy to pick up a copy, I will be out after the show and sign it for you." Well, with that offer, the line ran through the lobby and wound around the theater. Everyone had a story to

Jerry and Jack Ellsworth of WALK Radio (B. Grisafi Photo)

share with him, or wanted him to sign old, treasured albums, or posed for a photo with him. Jerry has always been gracious about such events and always enjoys meeting old friends and admirers.

In May of 1996, Jerry was honored by a special "Ellis Island Award" bestowed upon him by the National Ethnic Coalition of Italian Americans of the United States of America. "It's an organization that picks people from different backgrounds, for instance, anybody whose family came through Ellis Island into this country, whether it's your mother or father or even grandfather, and they choose people who are successful in their field - people who have done something for society or humanity - and my wife and I worked for the Heart Fund for a long time to raise money - also for the Cancer Fund - we did work for many different charities," Jerry said, "So when they asked me if I would accept this award as an outstanding Italian American citizen, I was pleased and proud to accept."

Here is Jerry Vale's take on his counterparts.

Frank Sinatra: While performing at the Sands, I worked alongside of one of my idols, Frank Sinatra, whose generous recommendation landed me the job in the first place. Frank and I remained unbroken friends until the day he passed away from us.

"Frank was always a gentleman and always made it a point to ask me if I needed anything, something he always and earnestly inquired of his friends. If we were performing in the same city, Frank would always extend an invitation for dinner or a party at his hotel suite. We would frequently appear together at Italian-American shows. Frank was consistently involved in supporting such projects. I sincerely miss him. He was the giant of our business, make no mistake about that."

Don Cornell: "When he and I were playing together in 2001 at Westbury, I could not believe how powerful his voice was, despite his handicap of not being able to perform standing up. He was amazing. Richard, you were there, am I right?"

Perry Como: "Well, you know-Como-beautiful voice-beautiful man-nobody ever came close to him as far as his outlook on life and the way he treats his family and his friends. He was just a beautiful guy."

Julius LaRosa: "I love Julie. He's been a dear friend for many years and he is one of the best singer's around. He's got the best feel of any singer. I mean, he can sing anything. He does jazz and he does it well."

Frankie Laine: "Frankie Laine is one of the most decent and lovable guys who sings differently than most of the others and has found great success with his style. He deserves it all. He was still singing when he was over 90 years old."

Tony Bennett: "I always love the way Tony performs. His heart is always in his voice. I am a *bona fide* Bennett fan, I would say, and have always followed his career, especially when we were both at Columbia. His career is still riding high."

Dick Haymes: "I thought Dick Haymes sang those low notes better than anyone. He had a good quality in his voice and when he hit those low notes, it was a pleasure to listen to them. A deep baritone, but he could also catch those high notes. He had quite a success, he made movies with Betty Grable - with Vivian Blaine - and Jeanne Crain - he did lots of good things. He had that problem because he was born in Argentina. They were talking

Jerry, Richard and Conductor Paul Mann before Westbury Concert, 2002
(R. Grudens Collection)

about deporting him at one time. It really hurt him but he stuck it out despite his problems. All these guys are my favorites."

Jerry Vale admires the great singers of the past as well. Al Bowlly, Mel Torme, Russ Columbo, and, of course, Bing Crosby.

Jerry's advice to up and coming singers is simple: "Just keep singing. If you keep doing it, someday - if the talent is really there - somebody will find you. Unfortunately, the way the world of popular music and entertainment works today, if you are not a rock artist it's hard to get records played unless you are working the nostalgic gigs. Sure, Sinatra, Como, Laine and myself are still played, but it's because we have established the territory and are well known enough and accepted by our countless fans."

Jerry was working concerts all over the United States when he had a mild stroke in 2002 while attending an autograph show in Los Angeles, that forced him to cut back his work for a while. Nevertheless, with a new spark of confidence and constant requests to perform in shows from Florida to Las Vegas, Jerry is considering a come back, so to speak.

"I don't know Richard, I am in an exercise program and have engaged a voice teacher to help restore my voice to it's old and perfected condition. If I can't bring it back up to speed, I may decide to retire, after all."

That subject is something Jerry and I spoke about at the last book signing we did together at Pomorodino's Restaurant in Hauppauge, New York. He was concerned about the constant flying and bus rides to venue after venue all over the map and thought he might reduce his work load to a restricted area, one where he could perform and be back to his home in Palm Desert the same, or next day. Engagements like those in Las Vegas or Los Angeles were on the list, but the East Coast was not.

Jerry's idea of a great day is to have lunch at Caffé Roma with his pals. They call themselves the Lunch Bunch, then they retire to the Playboy Mansion with friends Hugh Hefner, Chuck McCann, actor Robert Culp, Ray Anthony, Sid Caesar, Charles Durning, Harvey Korman, Dick Van Patten and Billy Shepard. There, they watch old movies and play poker while having dinner and talking over 'old times.'

With his cameo appearances in Martin Scorsese's *Casino* and *Goodfellas*, along with his appearances on the albums *Mob Hits* and *Mob Hits II*, Jerry is still earning a few bucks here and there. Columbia-Legacy has reissued his albums "I Remember Buddy" his tribute to Buddy Clark, and "I Remember Russ" a tribute to Russ Columbo, so Jerry is still selling records.

"I guess I've done pretty well over the years and am especially proud of my three performances at Carnegie Hall, in 1963, 1964 and in 1994. After my first show, the entire audience of about three thousand people joined me backstage at my invitation. The congratulations were endless. One by one the people, young and old, came up to me. I was so elated. I believe I clasped the hands of every single one of them - an unforgettable night of nights that capped my career. And I returned two more times to the same response."

AFTERTHOUGHT FROM JERRY VALE

"Many years have passed since my so-to-speak heyday, when my name as a performer was a household word. Now, at this time of my life, I am aware that my fans have been growing older along with me. Young adults may not know who Jerry Vale is, and why should they? They have their own musical heroes. However, at my last concerts many young adults attended, and for that I was grateful. I am also gratified for the legion of fans who have stuck with me throughout the years. That means you, dear reader."

You can find Jerry's name on the Hollywood Walk of Fame. It's been there since 1997.

Jerry Vale talks about his favorite foods:

"When Rita cooks at home, its pasta puttanesca with capers, olive oil and tomato sauce, as only she can make it. One of my favorite dishes is a variety plate of fresh orange roughy, swordfish, tuna and red snapper, usually with a mix of vegetables. Rita loves to make pasta of all kinds with sundried tomatoes and asparagus. Every one wants to be invited to my house for dinner and sooner or later they are."

Jerry Vale Records You Should Own

All of these records have been reissued on Sony-Legacy CDs:

"I Remember Russ" - Columbia CL 1164;
"I Remember Buddy" - Columbia CL 1114;
"Standing Ovation - at Carnegie Hall" - Columbia CS 9073;

and the great Jerry Vale Italian Album" - Columbia 30389

Selections:
Amore, Scusami (My Love, Forgive Me)
Rusella 'E Maggio
Oh, Marie
Vieni Su
Core'ngrato
Statte Vicine Amme
Passione (The Moments of Moments)
Non Ti Scordar Di Me
The Light of Roma
Tango Della Gelosia (Jealous of You)

Glenn Osser arranged and conducted these albums.

Recorded by PERRY COMO on RCA-Victor

CATCH A FALLING STAR

Words and Music by
PAUL VANCE and LEE POCKRISS

Pierino Como

Perry Como

"Mr. C." The Barber from Canonsburg

Perry Como and I go way back to the days of good old radio. He was working his durable pipes on a fifteen minute NBC show three nights a week in Rockefeller Center's Studio 6A. I was a very young studio page right out of high school, wearing one of those classy blue uniforms with a yellow braid over one shoulder and a monogrammed lapel pin in the shape of a microphone on the other. Perry and I would always exchange a few words before the show, about, of course, the show, and how many people might show up for the performance. "How we doin' tonight....anybody showing up?" he would cackle and grin. The studio was also the home of the weekly *Bell Telephone Hour*, a one hour program of classical and semi-classical music where outstanding vocalists like Ezio Pinza, of *South Pacific* fame, and the magnificent contralto Marion Anderson, performed.

Perry acquired lasting inspiration from performances of the great singers who preceeded him, Jolson, Crosby, Columbo, which he also talked about. His popular program was called *The Chesterfield Supper Club*, a show that later made a successful transition to television, unlike most radio shows, ran for 15 minutes and was similarly formatted and sponsored.

In those days, Perry was crooning his blockbuster hits "Till the End of Time," "A Hubba-Hubba-Hubba," "Because," "Some Enchanted Evening," and "Temptation." He had come a long way from those barber shop days in the small coal-mining town of Canonsburg, Pa. where, on May 18, 1912, he was born to Italian immigrant parents of twelve children. At the age of 14, he actually owned his own barber shop where customers always got their money's worth. Besides shaving and grooming them, he entertained by singing popular tunes. Then, in 1933, a musician, who was also a customer, and a member of Freddie Carlone's big band, carried an offer to him from Carlone for 28 dollars a week, singing and traveling with the band. Perry happily accepted and was on his way.

"I remember when Perry sang (later) for Ted Weems," Frankie Laine was telling me recently, "Perry was always a kind guy and got me a tryout with Freddie, just when I needed a job the most. But, sad to say, I didn't last but a few weeks....my music and style clashed with his." Perry and Frankie remained lifelong friends.

Perry traveled with the Weems band during the ensuing years perfecting his mellow vocal style. During World War II, the band had a hard time keeping together, so Perry simply returned to barbering back in Canonsburg. Encouraged by his childhood sweetheart, Roselle Belline, who remained his wife for over 60 years, Perry answered an offer from CBS to star in his own radio show. He returned to singing and signed his first recording  contract with RCA and released his first record, "Long Ago and Far Away." He remained with RCA for over 40 years, their longest running association with any artist. Perry amassed an enviable list of hits, 42 of them in the Top 10 between 1944 and 1958, second only to Bing Crosby.

Living in a small apartment in Long Island City, across the bridge from Manhattan, Perry was singing late-night performances at the Copacabana and taking the subway home after the 2:30 a.m. show.

During the 1950s it was "Don't Let the Stars Get in Your Eyes," "A Bushel and a Peck," "Papa Loves Mambo," "Catch a Falling Star," and "Wanted." Not bad!

Perry tried the movies but the big screen did not adequately project his personality, although he faired well enough in *Something for the Boys* in 1944 and *Doll Face* in 1945 and *Words and Music* in 1948, he became second in national popularity to his most admired rival, Bing Crosby, beating out Sinatra and Dick Haymes.

Perry Como turned to television in 1955 with *The Kraft Music Hall,* which he enjoyed very much more than making movies, and became the stunning star of a very high quality, hour-long variety show that lasted eight years. The "other" Ray Charles was his excellent choral director.

At the end of each show, Perry would sit perched on a simple stool in a cardigan sweater next to a music stand and just sing. His relaxed informality worked its way into millions of homes with songs like "Hot Diggity," "Round and Round," "Magic Moments," and silly tunes like "Delaware." Mitchell Ayres directed the orchestra with the Louis Da Pron Dancers and The Ray Charles Singers backing things up, while the Fontane sisters singing trio would sing:

"Letters, we get letters, we get stacks and stacks of letters. Dear Perry, would you be so kind to fill a request and sing the song I like best?" And, of course, Perry would answer the request for a thrilled listener or viewer.

Then came rock and roll and things changed in the music business. Perry reminded me that in 1970 it was composer Richard Rodgers who said: "This is the era of mediocrity. The kids can't play their instruments, they don't know anything about music, they buy a three dollar guitar and go in the bathroom and make a record and it sells nine million."

"It's crazy, but it's true," said Perry. "For years, singers like Vic Damone, Steve Lawrence, Jerry Vale, and others were unable to get recording contracts. Now, people like Tony Bennett are reinventing our kind of music, and thank God for radio and 'Music of Your Life' stations all over the country who still play our stuff."

In June of 1970, for the first time in 25 years, Perry Como appeared "live," and it was at the International Hotel in Las Vegas. Later that year, "It's Impossible" became his twentieth gold record. The songs "Seattle" and "And I Love You So" were also hits for Perry. At the age of sixty (he always looked thirty-five to me) he began a world tour. His *Forty Greatest Hits* album was a million seller in England, and did very well in Japan and Italy. His annual TV Christmas show became an American institution.

Perry, and Don Cornell Flank Harry Pezzullo
(Iris Cornell Collection)

In 1982, Perry performed to sell out concerts in Manila and Japan, and starred in a TV special from Paris for ABC with Angie Dickinson as his guest.

I remember once at a Westbury Music Fair concert on Long Island in 1986, a vendor in the theater lobby kept hawking magazines: "Seventy-two years old, fifty years in the business, buy a Perry Çomo book here!" Inside the arena style theater, Perry led off his concert with "The Best of Times" as he fielded himself from the runway to the in-the-round stage setting the tone for the evening.

Mickey Glass had been Perry Como's manager and overall business guardian for those 50 years and ran Perry's career from an office on Northern Boulevard in Great Neck, Long Island, with the help of Vera Hamilton, Perry's longtime secretary. "Perry doesn't like hectic things, but he likes the audience. They're his friends out there," Vera said, "and Perry is a genuinely nice guy."

When I sent Perry an article I had published that featured his friend Bing Crosby and the singers who followed him, Perry replied saying, "Bing was one of my idols in those early years. I used to imitate the Bing and Russ Columbo styles which were the most popular of that time in my career."

Then retired in Jupiter, Florida, where he played golf with old friends like Don Cornell, Perry said he missed his many New York friends, and "The only hair I cut now is for my grandchildren...but, they're terrible tippers." he grinned.

Perry would return to Long Island each year to participate in one of his charities, the St. Francis Hospital Celebrity Golf Classic.

I enjoyed the story that Jerry Vale told me recently about the time he visited Perry Como in Jupiter before Roselle passed away.

LOVING WORDS FROM JERRY VALE

"Opening the door in his bathrobe, he was happy to see me. We talked about lots of things for an hour or so. Upon leaving, he took me by the arm and walked me to my car. We embraced, and I left him, waving goodbye. If anybody had told me that someday my hero Perry Como, one of our very best singer's ever, would be walking me to my car in his bathrobe, I would not have believed it possible. Perry lost Roselle in 1998, and I know he was coping with his great loss as best he could. We lost Perry too, in 2001, six days short of his 89th birthday. It's so sad that we are losing all our friends, but we will always have his music."

Today, Perry's daughter, Therese, may be heard on

many radio stations across the land, lovingly featuring her dad's recordings and recounting family stories.

"I don't have a lot to tell you about myself, "Perry once told me," I did not lead an exciting life. I'm a singer and was once a barber but I stayed a singer. I'm a simple guy with simple tastes, that's what I tell everyone. That's all I can tell you."

Warm, melodious, pleasurable, personal : that's Perry Como. "The qualities that go into the making of a great pop singer are so changeable, so subject to the whims of fashion, that it is difficult to pin them down. Even within the context of a given period and a given style, the great pop singers are a complex mixture of voice, personality, sensitivity and taste - to mention just a few of the ingredients. Some singers find the key early and maintain it throughout their careers, as Bing Crosby did and Perry Como does...."

John S. Wilson
The New York Times
Sunday, June 5, 1983

HIS TEN BEST RCA ALBUMS

Critics contend these are his best albums.

DREAM ALONG WITH ME - CAMDEN 1957
COMO'S GOLDEN RECORDS - 1958
SATURDAY NIGHT WITH MR. C. - 1958
CHRISTMAS ALBUM - 1968 VERY BEST
IT'S IMPOSSIBLE - 1970
AND I LOVE YOU SO - 1973
LEGENDARY PERFORMER - 1976
I WISH IT COULD BE CHRISTMAS - 1982
PURE GOLD - 1984
TODAY - 1987

There were a few Best of Perry Como albums released in 1991 & '92 and a Collector's Edition in 1992 and a final album in 1993 entitled Yesterday and Today - A Celebration, all on RCA.

THAT LUCKY OLD SUN

(JUST ROLLS AROUND HEAVEN ALL DAY)

Lyric by
HAVEN GILLESPIE

Music by
BEASLEY SMITH

Recorded by **FRANKIE LAINE** on Mercury Records

Frank Paul Lo Vecchio

Frankie Laine - That Lucky Old Son.

Frank LoVecchio was born on March 30th on Townsend Street in the heart of Chicago's "Little Italy," the oldest of seven brothers and sisters. His parents, Anna and John LoVecchio, were from the village of Monreale, Sicily. His dad was a barber, and wanted Frank to be a pharmicist or architect. His mom wanted him to choose for himself. For various reasons the family moved to Siegel Street on Chicago's North side, then to Park Avenue, then to Schiller Street where they remained for twenty-five years. Frank sang in the choir of the nearby Immaculate Conception Church. Frank's first singing paycheck went to help his family.

Frankie Laine is indeed *That Lucky Old Son ever* since he first sang his way through his robust signature song "Lucky Old Sun" back in 1952. And, I am indeed his lucky Old *Step* Son, having been a friend for over 20 years ever since we first got together back in 1984. Since then he has been a true mentor, encouraging and nursing me through my first two books, *The Best Damn Trumpet Player* and *The Song Stars*, and working with me through this compilation of his fellow Italian singers. Frankie Laine celebrated his 91st birthday on March 29, 2004.

Frank is the author of his own autobiography, *That Lucky Old Son*, written with Joseph Laredo, with a prelude by the great biographical author, Irving Stone. This book is a personal walk through Frank's exciting and interesting career.

Back in 1997, I penned a book entitled *The Best Damn Trumpet Player* for which Frank wrote a touching and inspiring foreword. Included in the book is a chapter about Frank's career entitled *Mr. Rhythm - Frank Paul LoVecchio Takes the Mike.*

71

I BELIEVE

Words and Music by ERVIN DRAKE, IRVIN GRAHAM, JIMMY SHIRL and AL STILLMAN

Recorded by FRANKIE LAINE on Columbia Records

(Courtesy Ervin Drake)

I repeat it here verbatim and with a few additions, for your enjoyment:

It's difficult for me to believe that my friend Frankie Laine almost gave up on his fledgling singing career, actually taking off two and a half years to work at a defense plant where he earned a steady sixty-eight dollars a week. Then with a few bucks lined in his pocket, he returned to the fray to try once again, promising himself to quit if he did not meet with success on his next bid.

But, of course, he probably would not have stopped, no matter what he may have declared at the time. I think I know Frank pretty well now, and his determination and dedication to his craft were always unwavering, in good times or otherwise . Frank has conducted his personal and professional life admirably in every respect since his very first success in 1946 at that infamous Hollywood hangout on Vine Street, Billy Berg's, I'm sure, with dedication and his exemplary motivation, he would have hung on until his career turned itself around.

"I was invited to sit in one night and I came away with good luck for a change by singing "Old Rocking Chair's Got Me." My luck turned, because a guy in the audience got very excited about the way I sang it...and he turned out to be the song's composer, Hoagy Carmichael (the composer of "Stardust"), who got Billy (Berg) to give me a job." Frank grabbed the job that paid $75.00 a week.

Frank was the first *he-man singer*...other than country-western style singers - with whom the blue collar guys could identify, but he really had a hard time getting there with some bad luck along the way.

"Earlier, my friend bandleader Jean Goldkette got me a job at NBC, but England decided to declare war on Germany that day and my job went out the window. Hell, I was already 26 years old. I hung around Ted Weems' band while my pal, Perry Como, was his singer. Perry recommended me as his replacement when he was leaving, but Weems didn't accept it (Frank sang "Never in a Million Years" at his audition with Weems, that turned out to be prophetic) so Perry got me a job with his old boss, bandleader Freddie Carlone. This lasted just a few weeks because my singing style didn't match his Guy Lombardo type, sweet band.

"Frank's style was innovative, causing him difficulty with acceptance. He would bend notes and sing around the chordal context of a note rather that sing the note more directly like most singers of the day, and he stressed each rhythmic downbeat, another, different approach to traditional styles.

Singing at Cleveland's College Inn in 1940, Frank humanely introduced an unknown, literally starving singer, June Hart, who he really thought was terrific and needed a break. They actually *hired* her to *replace* him. Again, more bad luck while helping another. That's Frankie Laine. Some good luck occurred at that moment, for June sang "That 's My Desire," which Frank liked very much, which he filed in the back of his brain for six years.

"And how about the time I was ready to sing a benefit at the Congress Hotel in Chicago, when suddenly trumpeter Roy Eldridge showed up and decided to go into "Body and Soul?" Who in the world would dare interrupt that for a punk kid nobody even knew?" Fortunately, Frank later decided to try out his terrific version of "That's My Desire," with signature thrown back head, eyes closed, and mike in pleading hands, while at Billy Berg's. Well, it brought down the house and Frank finally began his climb to success. He began recording those great hits for Mercury and later for Columbia, (under the guidance of Mitch Miller) : "That's My Desire," "Lucky Old Sun," "Jezebel," "Mule Train," "Shine," "High Noon," "Cry of the Wild Goose," "Moonlight Gambler," and "Rawhide," all number one blockbuster hits, and to prove his bona fide allegiance to country music, how about his definitive interpretation of Hank Williams' "Your Cheatin' Heart."

What enthusiasm Frank instilled into every song he performed. But, as great as they are, I much prefer Frank's inspiring, early rendition of "We'll Be Together Again," which he wrote with his lifelong friend, Carl Fischer, and the prayer like, "I Believe," written by our mutual friend Ervin Drake. That song is Frank's personal favorite and actually an expression of his life's definition.

I first saw Frank perform at the New York Paramount in

Frankie and Friends

With Helen O'Connell

With His Mentor, Bing Crosby

With Richard Grudens

With Switzerland's Max Wirz - San Diego, 2004

With Mitch Miller at Columbia

1947. He was on the in-person bill with bandleader Ray McKinley and comedian Billy De Wolfe during the run of the Ray Milland/Marlene Deitrich film *Golden Earrings.* My first personal encounter with Frank was backstage at Westbury Music Fair where he was appearing with his discovery of long ago, Jimmy Dorsey song star Helen O'Connell, Moe Zudicoff (better known to all as bandleader Buddy Morrow, who fronts the Tommy Dorsey ghost band, Warren Covington and his then Pied Pipers, and the beloved William B. Williams, host then of New York's WNEW and its famous radio show *Make Believe Ballroom*, the long-running, classic disc jockey program that best represented all the performers of the Big Band Era. We hit it off like the old friends we later became. I felt I knew him since high school days. It was through his recordings that he made you feel that way. After talking awhile, we rounded up Helen O'Connell from her dressing room and cleared up how Frank first *discovered* Helen:

"Well, Jimmy Dorsey's secretary, Nita Moore, and I were having breakfast and she told me that Jimmy was looking for a girl singer. (Helen was nodding favorably to me). It happened that I saw Helen the night before singing at the Village Barn (night club) down on West Eighth Street and I told Nita about her and Jimmy went to see her that night, and that's how he got his singing star."

Helen, smiling, and now standing beside me posing for a photograph to be taken by my photographer, Camille Smith, who directed her to face me, saying, "Helen, look at Richard." Helen looked back at him and blurted coyly, "Do I have to?" That's Helen for you!

Frank recounted his phenomenal success when appearing in England, where he is so revered. On opening night at the Palladium, August 18, 1952, Frankie Laine broke the attendance record held previously by Judy Garland and Danny Kaye. He remained sold out for the entire two week engagement. Even the SRO spots were sold in record numbers the night of each show. Frank and his wife, Nan, were thrilled. It was more than ever expected. Crowds milled around the theater before and after each show hopeful to see the young singer.

During that run, Frank received a call from his A & R man

at Columbia, Mitch Miller, telling him that his recording of "Mule Train" and "High Noon" were released in the states and were an all out *smash.* Frank's manager and friend, Carl Fischer, improvised an arrangement from what he remembered of "Mule Train," and the next night they placed the song into the act. The audience responded wildly. Frank's version of "High Noon" is really the definitive, although it was Tex Ritter who sang the song on the film of the same name. People always expected to hear Frank when they viewed the film.

On to Glasgow, Scotland, Frank opened at the famed Empire Theater to an incredible reception. A crowd of over 5000 gathered outside their hotel and would not leave until Frank appeared on the balcony and sang a few bars of "Rock of Gibraltar," a song that went over big with U.K. audiences. Frank has always appreciated his fans.

Then on to Italy where he sang "Jezebel" to a screaming crowd, an event that occurred everywhere he traveled in his immigrant parent's place of birth. Appearances in Milan, Venice, Florence, and Rome, where crowds topped each previous performance, were equally exciting for the traveling performer from America. He and Nan were genuinely overwhelmed at all the attention given them. In France, where he renewed his friendship with singer Edith Piaf, known to the world as the *Little Sparrow,* Frank and Nan were followed by crowds of fans everywhere. "Jezebel" had been a big hit in Europe.

Frank returned to Europe over and over to even greater successes. He has recorded hundreds of titles over the years, and his international record sales exceeded the 100,000,000 mark long ago.

In his book *That Lucky Old Son,* Frank recalls that special feeling, corny though he thought it was, on returning a *success* to New York, where he once felt the lowest in his life. "I promised myself that I wouldn't come back to New York unless I could do so 'on a white horse'. "He could never forget the nights he slept on a bench in Central Park and the days that dragged by for him without even food to eat.

"That is why I made it a point to treat myself to one very special evening during my first run at the Paramount. I spent it alone. I donned a custom made suit and a camel hair overcoat and headed for Central Park. There, I sought out the dilapidated bench that had once been my bed. I sat down and ate a candy bar and thought about the time when penny candy bars were all I could afford to eat. In one of my pockets was a money loaded wallet, in the other, a key to one of the most comfortable hotel suites in New York. After a while, I hailed a taxi and drove to the heart of Times Square, where my name was lit up in big, beautiful lights where they were paying me $2,500 a week to do what I loved to do best." Frank hopes that everybody, at least once in their life, experiences such a moment.

In 1985, when I was writing a monthly column called *Jazz and Jazzmen* for Long Island PM Magazine, Frank fell ill, requiring a quadruple heart bypass operation. I informed my readers and invited them to write letters of encouragement to Frank at his San Diego hill top home that overlooks the harbor. He was typically so grateful.

Frank had a remarkable recovery and by the time 1990 rolled around, he had completed his fifth year since the surgery. In April, 1990 he had to have a triple bypass. In 1991 Frank was having throat troubles and took a year off all engagements. His wife, the former Nan Gray, had troubles with her vision, which was eventually fully restored.

Now, a few years later, with Nan gone, Frank continued performing benefits for Meals on Wheels, and other Human Health Services Agency programs that helped seniors, recorded a few new albums and attended book signings all over California to promote his autobiography.

"Nan's special way of touching my life will remain in my heart forever and lets me go on to do my work. I believe that God is everywhere. You don't have to go to a church to find him." Frank has one of the biggest hearts in show business and one of the smallest egos. Frank's final words in his book are, like the song says.."the music never ends." That's the best legacy Frankie Laine can ever give us.

Well, the above was written in 1997. After he lost Nan, his wife of 43 years, he summed up his life, saying," 'I Believe' sums up how I feel about life. God is everywhere. You don't have to go to church to find Him. For years, people have been writing to tell me how much they love the recording I made of ' I Believe'. It's my own favorite. It's a spiritual song that inspires people to have faith in themselves."

Since then Frankie married a long time friend Marcia Ann Kline, and still resides in his magnificent hilltop home overlooking San Diego Bay in California. It is here he displays his 21 gold records. We talk to one another and write regularly. Recently, Frank tried a Las Vegas comeback of sorts, but was not able to perform to his satisfaction, so, he retired from singing in public. He was 90 years old. What a run.

In 1998 Frank called, excited and buoyant, telling me of the release of "Wheels of a Dream," his brand new album. The album cover is a picture of Frank painted by non other than his friend, Tony Bennett.

In 2000 Frank performed a benefit with Benny Hollman and his Big Band, followed by an appearance at the Fallbrook Music Society in Fallbrook, California, another at the Orleans Hotel Showroom in Las Vegas. and two fall concerts at the Sun Coast Hotel in Las Vegas and at Scripps Cove in La Jolla, California. Not bad for a man of 87 years. In 2002, Frankie Laine fans learned of Frank's recorded CD of "The Story of Old Man Jazz and His Loves."

Frankie Laine's letter to all his fans and friends written on December 26, 2002 was a love note, a thank you, and an announcement of his 90th birthday bash in March of that year. The great day was celebrated at the U.S. Grant Hotel in San Diego to a "Rawhide" theme. The year was wrapped up with a premier showing of "An American Dreamer," a documentary of his legendary story on November 11, 2003, at the Museum of Photographic Arts in Balboa Park, California, hosted by Lou Rawls and vignettes by Dick Clark, Ringo Starr, Patti Page, Herb Jeffries, Maria Cole, Michel Legrand, Peter Marshall, John Williams, Shecky Greene, Clint Eastwood, Pat Boone, Mitch Miller, as audiences marched through the life of one of America's most popular male vocalists of all time.

I talked with Frankie Laine on Sept. 2, 2004, and he is doing just fine. Marcia, Frank and their French poodle Mattnoir had just finished posing for their 2004 Christmas card photo they will send to all their friends. I am honored to be one of their friends.

AUTHORS CHOICE - FRANKIE LAINES BEST

It's easy to choose Frankie Laine's hits, they are so distinctly his own. No one can sing "Cry of the Wild Goose," or "Jezebel" the way he does. There is no competition on most of his hits.

The "World of Frankie Laine" is currently available. It topped the charts in England in 1982 and has been re-issued. All his great songs are in it including "Lucky Old Sun."

"Portrait of a Legend," a re-issue of a 1992 Touchwood Records, "Memories in Gold," features contemporary remakes of most of Frank's gold hits.

In 1998 Touchwood released "Wheels of a Dream," Frank's first new studio recording in 20 years is a hit with some great new tunes for Frank, including "Song of India," "This Time the Dream's on Me," and the title song "Wheels of a Dream," that he does so well.

Readers Digest released a 3 CD boxed set of his music in May, 1997.

"It Ain't Over 'til It's Over," was produced in 1999 on CD and cassette.

The Frankie Laine Sicilian Octopus Salad

Prep time: 20 minutes
Cook time: 5 minutes
Ready in: 25 minutes

Ingredients:
1 can Italian olives, pitted
4 stalks celery, chopped
2 large carrots, chopped
1/2 cup extra virgin olive oil
2 lemons, juiced
6 gloves garlic, peeled and minced
1 sprig fresh parsley, chopped
salt and pepper to taste
3 pounds octopus, cleaned, cooked and sliced

Directions:

1.   In a medium bowl mix lemon juice, garlic and parsley. Season with salt and pepper.

2.   Bring a pot of water to a boil. Stir in octopus and cook about 3 minutes, or until tender; drain.

3.   Toss octopus, olives, celery, carrots and olive oil with the lemon juice mixture. Cover and chill in refrigerator until serving.

Make 12 servings

Enjoy!!

October 8, 1952

DOWN BEAT

Billy
Eckstine's
Own Story
(See Page 2)

★ ★ ★

Kenton Band
Revitalized
(See Page 2)

★ ★ ★

Johann's
Bach-Log
(See Page 4)

★ ★ ★

Steve Allen
(See Page 2)

★ ★ ★

On The Cover
Tony Bennett
(See Page 1)

25 cents

Society OF Singers News

Helping singers through times of crisis

SOS PROUDLY PRESENTS TONY BENNETT WITH THE 9th Ella Lifetime Achievement Award

at the Beverly Hilton Hotel Sunday February 6, 2000

83

Anthony Dominick Benedetto

Tony Bennett

The Other Saloon Singer, Who Still Sings Today.

The first time I met Tony Bennett, I was being detained by theater security when Tony comes forward and calls out to me, "Hey! Richard," and he waved me through," C'mon over, I've been waiting for you."

Well it was an extremely cold evening and Tony was waiting to go on. We had made a date for an interview, but his people never left my name at the door. Tony, however, true to everyone else's image of him, rescued me and we had our long conversation and even took some photos. That was in 1986.

Since then, instead of a diminishing career, Tony Bennett's star spiraled upward, thanks in part to his son Danny, who took on his management: "My career was never at a standstill. It just may have seemed that way, because I was performing just like always, and everywhere. It just made the back page because all the rock stars took center stage over the last few years. But my fans are civilized and my following is now stronger than ever."

In 1988, a chapter covering his career appeared in *American Singers* by Whitney Balliett. In 1997, Tony was a subject in my book *The Best Damn Trumpet Player*, and in 1998, in a book dedicated to his mom, entitled *The Good Life*, written with his good friend Will Friedwald, Tony has been well covered in print over the years. Tony Bennett credits all the old songwriters for his success. "It's not whether a song is new or old that makes it great...it's whether it's bad or good that makes a song live or die."

He never gets tired of singing the worthy strains of Irving Berlin, Cole Porter, Harold Arlen, George Gershwin, or Harry Warren. He has a sort of instinct for selecting the songs that suit him. In the case of his immensely popular gem "I Left My Heart in San Francisco," he recalls that while rehearsing it with his piano accompanist Ralph Sharon in a Hot Springs hotel bar before he first introduced it at the Fairmont Hotel in San Francisco, "A bartender was listening and, after we finished rehearsal, he told me he would *enthusiastically* buy a copy if we ever recorded it. That was the first tip-off that we had a hit in the making. Right up to today, it's still my biggest request - it gets the best reaction, and San Francisco is really a beautiful city - it's a musical city - and I love to sing about it." The recording won a Grammy.

Some argue the song is too sentimental and weak, but it brings in the faithful and will probably be the song with which he will always be identified, happily or not.

While we talked backstage, Sarah Vaughan was on stage singing and he was slated to follow her. We could hear her over the speakers loud and clear. "What a magnificent background for our interview, listening to Sarah." Tony said. Tony makes an art out of feelings: "I conjure up emotion much like the impressionist artists who work with light. Feelings are the opposite of coldness...I try to sing in a natural key...choosing strong lyrics with meaning...then I inject my own feelings into it."

It's more than feelings that drive Tony Bennett. Ever since he won an Arthur Godfrey Talent Scouts Contest, coming in second to Rosemary Clooney, Tony's career has always expanded, helped by a battery of million sellers, namely "Because of You," "Rags to Riches," "Blue Velvet," Cold, Cold Heart" and "Boulevard of Broken Dreams."

It was Bob Hope who told me that it was he who changed Tony's early stage name of Joe Bari to Tony Bennett because he thought *Bari* sounded phony. Hope had invited Tony to join his show at the New York Paramount after hearing him sing at the Village Barn in Greenwich Village, in lower Manhattan, where he was appearing with Pearl Bailey. "Right there and then at the Paramount Bob announced what would be my new name and told me I was going on tour with him all over the U.S. - it was great. Who could argue with Bob Hope?"

Tony was brought up in a non-affluent Manhattan suburb known as Astoria. His father passed on when he was 10, and his mom had to support the family. Uncles and Aunts helped feed that family of four in those hard times. "It was a warm feeling among all of us, and I would sing for the family on Sunday's"

Tony loves to be associated with Sinatra, Armstrong, Ellington and others of the swinging years: "Why between them they've written played and sung more music than anyone. They all will go down in music history as being as important as Beethoven or Bach."

Richard and Tony, Westbury Music Fair - Back Stage (C. Smith Photo)

With Tony Bennett, every show is his last show. When he had to record what record executives wanted back in the 1950s, he did it and luckily succeeded. But since then he chooses his own tunes to record with the assistance of his longtime musical director and pianist Ralph Sharon.

"I would get record execs angry at me when I would not record some of the garbage, so they labeled me a fanatic and troublemaker. I considered that a compliment. They were forcing artists to take a dive. Remember, they are accountants and marketing guys and don't know or care about the product." Over the years Tony has matured into a more disciplined performer who communicates with his audience and never really ever sings a song the same way twice, one of the things I love about his performances.

Whitney Balliett: "Bennett is an elusive singer. He can be a belter. He drives a ballad as intensely and intimately as Sinatra. He can be a lilting jazz singer. He can be a low key, searching supper-club performer. But Bennett's voice binds all his vocal selves together. His voice has a joyous quality, a pleased, shouting-within quality."

As a young man, Tony was trained to be a commercial artist at Manhattan's School of Industrial Arts. "But, I always had to sing. It was something in my genes..my Italian heritage. I have spent my whole life studying and thinking about my singing. My whole family sang, too."

Tony was influenced early by the school's choral director. He joined the chorus to learn his craft, and, after singing with military bands while serving in the armed forces in Europe, he came home and entered the American Theater Wing professional school under its director, Miriam Spier. While studying, he rounded out a livelihood by playing club dates around

Richard and Sarah Vaughan
(C. Smith Photo)

Manhattan and even served as an elevator operator at the Park Sheraton Hotel to make ends meet.

Tony Bennett also credits Art Tatum's ingenious piano playing and Mildred Bailey's jazz voice as mentor's. In 1986, shortly after the time of my first interview with him, his *The Art of Excellence* album was doing pretty well on the charts: "Listen to this," Tony declared over the telephone from Atlantic City when I called to congratulate him, "It's number

Tony with Harold Arlen (Sam Arlen Collection)

one...and it's wonderful...and to think it's in front of the Rolling Stones and the great Bruce Springsteen. It's full circle for me." The album, still available, contained an amazing duet with the late, great Ray Charles on James Taylor's "Everybody's Got the Blues" and a number called "City of Angels," which was written by Fred Astaire, plus my favorite of the album, an almost forgotten song from Irving Berlin's *Annie Get Your Gun,* "I Got Lost in His Arms." In 1993, his album entitled *Perfectly Frank,* a tribute to Frank Sinatra, but in the Bennett mold, won a Grammy.

Speaking of Grammy's, Tony's 1994 Album *Tony Bennett: MTV Unplugged* won another Grammy. It was the biggest selling album of Tony's long career. It was actually nominated for three Grammy's, including Album of the Year. Tony was sixty-eight. "And, I did it without compromising my music," he said. In 1995, paying tribute to all the lady singers, Tony's album *Here's to the Ladies,* won another Grammy for Best Traditional Pop Album.

Up to 1999, Tony Bennett had won eight Grammy's. In 2003, another Grammy for *Playin' With My Friends,* composed of duets with B.B. King and Sheryl Crow. According to B.B. King, "To work with this man is a great highlight of my life. I've met two presidents and the Pope, Pavorotti - and now Tony Bennett."

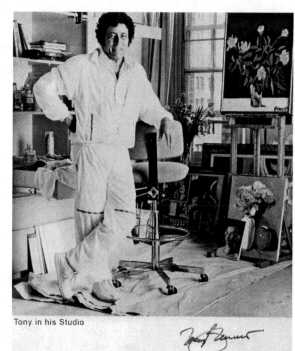

Tony Bennett is another kind of artist, for you readers who do not know this. Tony is a portrait and landscape artist. He signs his works *Benedetto* and sells them all over the world, which is where he paints his subjects on canvas between shows and while on tour. I saw a handful of them at Westbury Music Fair where they were on display during a show he

Tony in his Studio

performed with Rosemary Clooney. They were mostly cityscapes and landscapes. From my interview with Tony one evening a few years later, I was able to write a piece for an art magazine about his art alone.

> Bob Hope used to tell Tony some good advice: "Come out smiling, show the people you like them."
>
> "To this day, I still follow that rule. Some performers say they don't care if the audience likes them or not. With that philosophy, they should stay home."

Tony's kids, Danny, who brought his dad into the current scene via MTV, Daegal, a recording engineer and producer; Joanna, an actor and art designer, and Antonia, now 29, a graduate of the Berklee School in Boston, who is breaking into a singing career of her own, remain the true loves of his life. They have furnished him with some beautiful grandchildren. There exists a world famous Hirschfield cartoon depicting *A Group of America's Great Artists,* "There's Ella, Bing, Nat Cole, Fred Astaire, Judy Garland, and I'm in that group. I can't believe it, but it's true. When you first start painting, or doing anything, and it doesn't work out, you're devastated. But you keep painting. Then you're not bothered by your mistakes. You just say, 'The next time will be better.' That's what happens in life. That's why I wouldn't change anything, because I made mistakes, but those mistakes taught me how to live, and boy, am I living."

Part of living for Tony Bennett is sharing. Tony's support for the Juvenile Diabetes Foundation and donating his art to front the American Cancer Society's Christmas Cards is just some of the work he does for others.

Tony has recently won his twelfth Grammy for Best Traditional Pop Album *A Wonderful World* performing duets with his long time singing partner and friend, k.d.Lang, that contain the many favorite standards he loves to sing. The album is dedicated to his cherished friend, Rosemary Clooney, featuring her own "Tenderly." Tony has long past the 50 million record sales mark. Look for Tony as he tours America, Canada and London in 2005 and beyond.

Authors Choice -The Best Recordings of Tony Bennett

We have selected a list of albums we think are the very best material offered by Tony Bennett. They are our own personal favorites. These albums reflect most of the important works he recorded.

I love the original Tony Bennett album *Because of You,* released in 1952 because it contains my Bennett favorites: "Because of You," "Boulevard of Broken Dreams," and "Cold, Cold Heart." They are the evergreen and unmistakable Tony Bennett cry. I remember when I was at NBC in 1952, and "Because of You" was the number one hit. You could hear it played in those narrow record stores along Broadway and on 42nd Street over loudspeakers. I have to recommend the 1951 single "Blue Velvet" as Tony's best single. It was also his mother's and Ella Fitzgerald's favorite Bennett recording. Over the years, much of his material was reissued over and over.

In the 1960 album *More Tony's Greatest Hits*, "Smile," "Put on a Happy Face," "Love Look Away," and "Firefly" are dominant and great.

I have made it an emotional rule not to enjoy the re-recordings of an artist's original recordings. This also applies to Tony. The originals to me are the best material, often guided by his early producers like Mitch Miller. Reissues are ok, but new versions of the old songs are not as cherished.

Other individual recordings I enjoy by Tony are Just in Time, 1956; "I Left My Heart in San Francisco," 1962: "I Wanna Be Around, 1962: The Good Life," 1963: "Maybe This Time, 1972: and "O Solo Mio," 1973-his rare Italian recording: It's funny, but Tony Bennett never sang any of the standard Italian American song book.

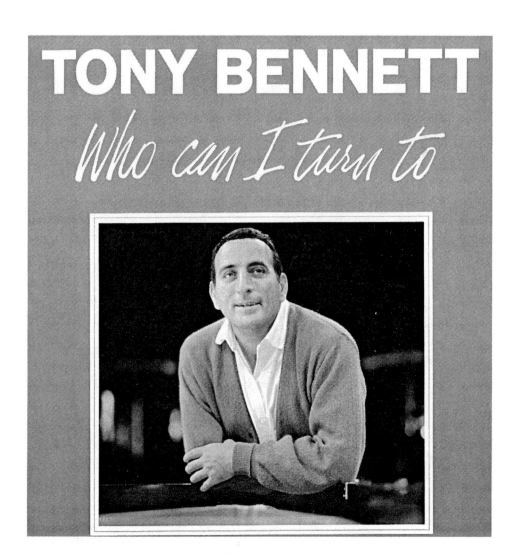

TONY BENNETT

Who can I turn to

EH, CUMPARI!

Adaptation by JULIUS LA ROSA and ARCHIE BLEYER

AS RECORDED BY JULIUS LA ROSA ON CADENCE RECORD No. 1232

JULIUS LA ROSA

ROSARCH PUBLISHING CORP.

Julius La Rosa

JULIUS LA ROSA

Proud of His Italian Roots

When Julius La Rosa and I got together during the summer of 1999, we discovered we lived but a few blocks from one another during the mid-1940s, in Brooklyn, New York, where you could always find me glued to my three-speed Admiral phonograph playing mostly Bing while Julie was dreaming of singing like his hero Frank Sinatra.

"In Grover Cleveland High School I was the vocalist with the school dance band. We sang mostly dance charts. Then I heard Sinatra. Before him a singer was just an adjunct to a band - always singing in tempo, never paying much attention to the lyrics. Sinatra taught me that songs are really little poems. He was the first to put a comma here, a hyphen there, three dots here, and a period there. What he was doing was telling the story as he interpreted it. Before that, a singer sang (he sings) *I love you truly* - but Frank sang (Julie sings again) *I love you-tru-ly,* giving the words meaning-interpreting the song the way the composer intended. Ask any singer my age and they will tell you that Sinatra was their major influence."

Julie, as he likes to be called, joined the Navy after high school and wound up in Pensacola, Florida aboard a ship as an electronics technician. Arthur Godfrey (a great CBS radio personality, emcee of the *Arthur Godfrey Show* on both radio and television) was there earning his Navy "Wings" which meant he had to qualify by landing and taking off from an aircraft carrier six times.

"Someone," said Julie, "to this day I don't know who it was - probably a kid in my division - got word to him to catch me singing at the enlisted men's club. He did, and I sang 'The Song Is You' and 'Don't Take Your Love from Me." After the show he said to me, 'When you get out of the Navy, look me up-I've got a job for you.'" Julie followed through, and on exactly November 19, 1951 he began singing on the very popular Arthur Godfrey radio show. "I had no show business experience, so the six months I spent on the radio gave me a chance to get comfortable before I was to join the television program. And, God bless bandleader Archie Bleyer, he was my major influence. He saw that I was just a kid, so he took me under his wing."

Archie Bleyer converted Julie into a professional singer: "My first hit was unexpected. The song 'Anywhere I Wander' had been recorded by Tony Bennett, Mel Torme, and others - remember in those days everyone would record the same song, but nobody had a hit with it. I liked the song. It was from the film *Hans Christian Andersen,* and sang it on the radio show and the Wednesday night TV show a couple of times. We got mail asking where to buy the record, but I wasn't recording at the time. That's when Archie decided to start Cadence Records."

The first Cadence recording "Anywhere I Wander" became a big hit for Julie. "Yes," Julie said, "and the record catalog number was 1230 - a number I'll never forget for two reasons. 1-2-30 is both my birthday and the catalog number of my first recording."

Another big hit for Julie was the serendipitous and charming "Eh, Cumpari," a Sicilian folk song similar in structure to "Old McDonald Had a Farm" with instruments instead of animals. "It was a song I sang as a kid. 'Eh Cumpari' means - well, you get married and you ask a friend to be best man - you are *cumpari*. It's a very close relationship between two people . A friend has a child - you are asked to be Godfather - we are now *cumpari*," Julie explained. Julie had lots of fun recording that song. It was an infectious tune something like Rosemary Clooney's "Come-on-a-My House" ditty that made her so famous.

EH, CUMPARI!
Transcribed by Julius La Rosa and Archie Bleyer
Eh, cumpari!
(Eh,cumpari)
Ci,vo'sunari - chisi sona?
(Let's make some music)
(What'll I play?)
'U friscalettu
(The piccolino)

E comu si sona
(But how do you play it)
'U frisealettu?
(The piccolino?)
(whistle) 'U friscale tt'e
Tipiti tipiti ta
(two more verses)
The saxophona and the Mandolino
Other words repeated

Julie recounted a very amusing story about his trip to Italy: "I was visiting my uncle in Palermo, Sicily and asked to see where my father was born. He took me to an area of the city comparable to what we in New York call *Hell's Kitchen.* When I got back to the hotel I sent my dad a telegram: 'Dad, saw where you were born. Glad you moved.'"

Julie's dad was the quintessential radio repair man. He opened and closed a number of shops during his life, eternally searching for that *better*, more lucrative location. "He was known as Charlie, the Radio Man," Julie said.

Okay, everyone, here is what you've been waiting for, the true story about how Julie dealt with his *famous firing on the air* by his boss, Arthur Godfrey:

"Well, I broke a rule. I hired a manager. You could not have a manager when you worked on the Godfrey Show. Godfrey had called CBS Chairman William Paley and told him my new manager, Tommy Rockwell of General Artists, informed him that in the future all dealings with Julius La Rosa had to go through his office. I've been told Paley said to Godfrey, 'You hired him the air - so fire him on the air.' and Godfrey did exactly that while millions were watching." The date: October 4, 1953.

After singing the song "Manhattan," Arthur Godfrey summarily *executed* Julius La Rosa: *"That was Julie's swan song with us. He goes out on his own now, as his own star, to be seen on his own show. Wish him Godspeed, as I do,"* he announced in a matter-of-fact tone.

LaRosa Whips Jitters To Win On Voice Alone

Chicago—Julius LaRosa now has been away from the Arthur Godfrey nest slightly more than a year. The handicappers who gave him less time than this on his own can return to their scratch pads and guess again. He has put one thing under his belt in that period— and it's important in a business where a quick demise is closer to the rule than to the exception.

He has found that an audience wants to hear him sing, not to look for his humility. At the Chicago theater where he played a three-week engagement last month with Kitty Kallen co-headlining, his stint classified as *smash* at the box-office—and most of this had happened before the latest installments to his private life were documented on the newspaper front pages.

'On My Own Merits'

"From here on," says LaRosa, "I want to score on my own merits." Actually the "freak status" (his own term), which the newspapers gave him, is a lot to overcome for a performer who is not as concerned with the immediate buck as with the long term.

He's been helped no little by his accompanist-arranger, Joe Guercio, who in the past had worked with Patti Page, Norman Brooks, and Georgia Gibbs.

Onstage, LaRosa doesn't tug his trouser leg anymore, doesn't scratch his head, or rub his nose boyishly —all the things that once were construed as a show of shyness and, that awful word, humility.

'A Show of Nerves'

"Humility," he says, "had nothing to do with it. Man, this was just a show of nerves by a guy who was scared and didn't know how to hide it. But I'm over it now. I've got much more confidence, and that's a big step forward."

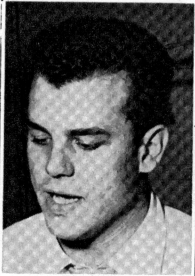

Julius LaRosa

LaRosa has been a long time looking for his true vocal identity. The first complication was that he sounded much like Frank Sinatra and, accused of imitating, he spent a long period trying to sing as much unlike the man as possible. He was never comfortable at it, so he went back to what comes naturally.

"Now if I sound a little like Sinatra," he says, "I don't mind it. In fact I call it a blessing, because I really dig that man. Eventually I should develop a technique that is both natural and all my own, but right now I can stand the resemblance to the greatest there is."

—les

(Courtesy Metronome Magazine)

"Did you say anything to Godfrey afterwards?" "Yes. After the show I thanked him for giving me my break. It was all cordial, no rancor. In an interview many years later Godfrey said: 'The only SOB that ever said *thank you* was that kid, La Rosa.'"

So the young and handsome singer Julius La Rosa began performing in clubs and theaters all over the country.

"I worked where they still had live shows and had to learn my job in front of the public, that is, how to control an audience, what tools to use, what *taste* was."

Since then Julie has done it all, from singing with the Glenn Miller Orchestra with current leader Larry O'Brien to sharing the billing on stage live with the great First Lady of Song, Ella Fitzgerald. "In fact, she was the 'extra added attraction.' Can you imagine that?"

Once, executives tried to make a rock-type idol of Julie via a movie entitled *Let's Rock* with Paul Anka and Danny and the Juniors. It didn't work.

"I will someday find a print of that film and burn it," quipped Julie. It was the only movie he ever made.

In 1969, Julie took a job with New York's WNEW-AM radio where he talked, played recordings, and hosted musical guests weekdays from one to four until 1977, when the station changed hands.

"It's a whole different thing when you have to sit in front of a mike for four hours at a clip. The entire show was done *ad lib* - totally spontaneous. I enjoyed every minute. I learned while I worked and people listened. I loved working alongside the great William B. Williams, Ted Brown, and my friend, newscaster Mike Prelee." In 1997, Julie was a guest on Mike's radio show *In the Spotlight* on New Jersey radio.

For La Rosa listening, we can recommend one of his best albums *Better Than Ever* on Candlewood Records. Here, the musicians are well chosen: Tenor-alto Ted Nash, bass of David Finck, Gene Bertoncini and Bucky Pizzarelli's guitars, and conducted by Bill Waranoff, who also arranged. Julie is very animated on the songs "Just in Time" and "Something's Got to Give." On the serious side there is "Here's That Rainy Day Again." "My Foolish Heart," an old favorite is on this album to enjoy.

MOBILE

Words and Music by BOB WELLS and DAVID HOLT

JULIUS LA ROSA

Recorded by JULIUS LA ROSA on Cadence Record No. 1251

PRICE
50¢
(in U.S.A.)

ARDMORE MUSIC CORP.
1730 BROADWAY, NEW YORK, N.Y.

Recently, when Jack Ellsworth of radio station WALK on Long Island played Julie's rendition of "Once to Every Heart" on his daily show *Memories in Melody,* many listeners called in and wanted to know where to get the recording.

"My fans are civilized and loyal," Julie says, and thank God for those wonderful people. They allow a lot of us singers a way to make a living for which I am grateful.

Julie lives up along the Hudson River, close to Manhattan, with his wife Rory, in a split level house. "If I hadn't married this lady, I'd be on a funny-farm today. We have two great kids who aren't kids anymore. Chris is an acoustic engineer who was born on the fourth of July. Till he was five he thought all the annual fireworks were always displayed for him. Our Maria, actually Maria Lucia Teresa La Rosa Smith graced us with a grandchild who is now seven, completing our family tree."

Julie and I favor different baseball diamonds, he rooting for the New York Mets and I for the New York Yankees, although we both started out as Brooklyn Dodger fans, that is, until they uprooted the team and moved to the West coast in 1957. We'll never forgive them.

Whether Julius sings "Eh! Cumpari" or "Anywhere I Wander," or any other Sammy Cahn or Harold Arlen tune, or any good song, he effectively places these songs directly into your heart.

In August of 2004, Julie sang his heart out during a Las Vegas engagement, and plans to spend November 2004 through May 2005 headlining a review in Palm Desert, California, called "Senior Class" with Anna Marie Alberghetti, Ruta Lee, and Ralph Young. That should keep him busy singng his favorite songs for a while.

Spiedini A La Julius La Rosa

1/2 lb. loin of pork (thin slices)
1/2 lb. boned breast of chicken (cubed)
1/4 lb. pork livers (thinly sliced)
6 baby lamb chops
sage, rosemary, salt (to taste), freshly ground black pepper
1/2 cup olive oil
4 Juniper berries

On metal skewers, alternate arrangements of chicken, pork, liver, lamb and bacon on each skewer. Place in roasting pan and sprinkle spices over them. Also pour oil over and toss in Juniper berries.

Marinate for six hours. Before cooking, make sure meat is well covered with seasoning and oil. Cook over an open fire, or very hot broiler. Cook for approximately 15 minutes - turn frequently.

May be prepared ahead but does not freeze well.

A painstaking recipe which Julius' mother makes for him. His sister, Sadie, always teases Mama about making spiedini for him, the baby, but "...not for me!"

Serves 4 - 6

Richard!
It's
a
pheasure!
Julie
Lacksor

Don Cornell

IT ISN'T FAIR ★ I'M YOURS ★ I WALK ALONE ★ HOLD MY HAND
12 GOLD RECORDS

102

Luigi Francisco Varlaro

Don Cornell

BIG VOICE, BIG HEART

It was always hard to tell who had the most enthusiasm in the Cornell family, Don or Iris. That enterprising couple had worked very hard to insure that a new generation, as well as reminding the previous one, got to hear the man with the big voice, long-respected big band vocalist, and later singing icon, Don Cornell.

Richard and Don 2001, Westbury

Don and I met only once, but it was a long enough meeting backstage at Westbury Music Fair during a Don Cornell-Jerry Vale joint concert performance in 2001. He was still a handsome, engaging performer then, dressed in tux and ready to take on the audience of over 3000 fans.

"He still sings in the same key as when he was young," a bubbly Iris said. Iris was Don's greatest fan.

"After losing my first wife edith to cancer after 36 years of marriage, I was dejected and had no desire to perform. Iris changed all that for me in 1978, when we were married," Don was saying, "she's been managing things successfully for over 20 years now. I consider myself twice blessed."

In concert, when Don sang "The Wind Beneath My Wings," it's clearly dedicated to Iris, "....singing it as if only she were in the room," wrote Anthony DeFlorio, III in a review earlier when Don appeared at Resorts International in Atlantic City. "Don always meant every word of it, ending with a powerful flourish. Even though she must have heard it many times before, Iris was always moved, as was the audience," Anthony concluded.

My recollection of Don's hit "It Isn't Fair," recorded with the Sammy Kaye orchestra in 1950, convinced me of his ability to put over a song and make it a hit, as he clearly accomplished with this great 1933 Richard Himber theme song.

Stepping back a bit, Don first began to sing in local clubs in the Bronx, New York, and playing guitar and singing with the Mickey Alpert band at the Edison Hotel in New York City in the 1930s. "I also played and sang with the McFarland Twins, the sax playing brothers who had their own band, and with Lennie Hayton's orchestra."

Don sang with Loring "Red" Nichols and His Five Pennies, too. His singing *teachers* were Bing Crosby and Russ Columbo: "We all looked up to Bing as the singer who started it all. My first record date was with the Bobby Hayes' band vocalizing "Trust in Me," later a big hit for Eddie Fisher."

Don was born of immigrant parents on Mott Street and moved to the Bronx. "We had no radio, so we entertained ourselves. My father played the mandolin. Mom sang in the church choir, so on Sunday we had a family sing-a-long which included my four brothers. It was instilled in us as in so many other Italians."

He acquired the name of *Don Cornell* very simply. "It was difficult to sell a name like Lou Varlaro in show business in those days, especially since Italy's dictator Mussolini had joined the Axis Countries with Hitler during the second World War. Every time they called out my name there would be some boo's from the audience." So, one night I was standing in the wings, and Sammy Kaye called out, 'Now, here's Don Cornell,' and I'm looking around thinking, 'who the hell is that?' And, Richard, that is how it all started." Don spoke like he sang - clear and strong.

Don broke into the big time beginning in 1950 with the Sammy Kaye, *Swing and Sway* backed recordings "It Isn't Fair," "Daddy," "Harbor Lights," "Serenade of the Bells," and one of my Don Cornell favorites, "Stage Door Canteen." Here Don was able to utilize his pulsating, powerhouse voice to propel the band from being what they called a mild "*Mickey Mouse*" style band into a more respectable, versatile and assertive member of the Big Band community.

"With Sammy," Don recalled, "we had an itinerary that ran from January to January, with only one week off for Christmas." Don left Kaye to perform military service with the Army Air Corp., then later rejoined the band.

The tune "Heart of My Heart," recorded with fellow vocalists Johnny Desmond and Alan Dale, was always a big request song for Don at concerts. Don has a Gold Record for each year from 1950 through 1962. "The first, 'It Isn't Fair,' is the most requested, followed by the Coral recording 'I'm Yours,' Don said, "and we engage a full orchestra so we are able to retain the original charts when I do these requests. The fans always expect to hear the original versions."

Don recounted a little yarn about the original release of "It Isn't Fair."

"Unaware of the record release, I drove up to a concert date and found lines around the block. I literally had to fight my way into the building. I discovered the recording was just released and was being featured on many disc jockey shows around the country. Boy, what a surprise, and what crowds filled each show after that day." "Hold My Hand," another big Cornell hit, one that became a #1 hit in England and remained on the charts for 21 weeks, was featured in the 1954 movie *Susan Slept Here.* It received an Academy Award nomination, unfortunately to be eclipsed by a luckier entry "Three Coins in the Fountain."

Let's hear it for *time and chance!*

Don excels on so many great recordings: "I'll Walk Alone," "That Old Feeling," "Most of All," "The Bible Tells Me So," (by Roy Rogers and Dale Evans) "Play Some Music for Broken Hearts," "When I was a Child," "Most of All," and "Love is a Many Splendored Thing." Don's classic baritone has remained in demand for all the ensuing years and right through 2003, something he never expected.

"I have always believed a song tells a story. It must be interpreted through feelings," Don said during our meeting, "the message must be conveyed by the singer to the listener. That's how it's done."

Don usually closed his concerts with a tune called "Old Man Time:"

"That song was given to me by my dear friend Jimmy Durante. My first job after leaving Sammy (Kaye) in 1950 was at Palumbo's in Philadelphia, where all the big names performed. I was on the bill with Durante. On about the third day he called me into his dressing room and said, 'I have a song for you. I want you to take it and put it away and don't sing it for forty years. You're too young to understand it now.' If you check the lyrics, you can understand what he was trying to tell me."

"He gives you youth and he steals it away,

He gives you nice pretty hair and turns it gray."

"Yes. I only remember Jimmy Durante singing it, so I put it in my act. It's always a very personal experience each time I sing it," Don said.

"And the audiences absolutely adore it," added Iris. Like Kay Starr loves to sing "Wheel of Fortune," and Tony Bennett loves to do "I Left My Heart in San Francisco," Don loves "It Isn't Fair." "You owe allegiance to those songs," Don said quite seriously. "Don't you ever get tired of singing it over and over?" I asked. "Well, I've been doing it for fifty years and it's my trademark. My album *From Italy With Love* contains many more of the favorites I enjoy singing. Here you'll find my original Italian favorites "Mala Femmena," "Ciao, Ciao Bambina," "Volare," and "Non Dimenticar."

Singing those timeless Italian ballads are my favorite time at a concert and the audience responds so favorably to these endearing melodies."

Iris Cornell Speaks

"Don's releases in the late nineties were so well received - igniting a rebirth of his career. The albums *From Italy With Love, Something to Remember Me By,* and *I'll Be Seeing You* scored so well. It was rewarding to watch his career take off again through these CDs. People called us from all over the country to order them and radio stations everywhere played them regularly. It was so exciting for us at the time."

Those albums were digitally remastered from the original '50s and '60s recordings and were drawn from the multi-labels including Coral and RCA. Iris sent me a copy of each album, and she was right. "And remember Richard, some of the musicians and arrangers on those originals were among the finest craftsmen ever involved in music."

JUNE, 1998.

Asking Don for spontaneous comments with respect to his peers, he said exactly this: Sinatra is considered the Chairman. Perry Como and I have been friends for almost 60 years. He has his Rose, and I have my Iris," he says with a broad smile.

"We'll be playing golf together this Tuesday. It's funny, but true - Perry and I joined the big bands around the same time when he started with Freddie Carlone. The whole world loves Perry. **Tony Bennett** is also a great stylist - but although he never sang with the bands, he certainly is a dynamic performer. **Mel Torme** is a brilliant composer and a great artist. **Jimmy Roselli**? Jimmy is one of the greatest Italian singers around. **Guy Mitchell**? I love Guy Mitchell.

Jerry Vale - I know Jerry many, many years and we often work together. **Frankie Laine** and I did a concert together a few months ago. He's another fine singer, as is **Julius LaRosa**. The best thing that ever happened to Julie is when he got fired by Godfrey. **Dean Martin**? Dean once said that everything he learned as a singer he learned from me. I'm proud of that."

If Don Cornell had to begin all over again: "I would have used my big voice more, but everybody was crooning then, so I had to go along with the wave." Don would have applied the power he performs with today, as he does with his emotionally powerful version of "I'll Walk Alone." Nobody does it better.

"Don simply walks onto center stage in his inimitable way, greets his audience, sings and, guess what? He owns the room - every inch of it," wrote author Joseph Laredo for Don's album *Something to Remember Me By*.

Now, with Don's passing, the album becomes another legacy.

Laredo continued: "We feel pangs of nostalgia when we realize that Don Cornell was probably the last of the reigning crooners who began as a boy singer with the Big Bands of the 1930s and 1940s...." and may I add "who was still singing in the year 2003."

On Monday, February 23, 2004 Don Cornell passed from us at Adventura Hospital from advanced emphysema and diabetes. Don was a lifelong smoker who just wouldn't quit. I remember his last appearance with Jerry Vale on May 19, 2001. On stage he sat upon a stool and held the mike stand. His voice was no different than the early Don Cornell, but his legs would not hold him for the required hour. Back in the dressing room, along with his assistant Zora, his wife Iris, Jerry Vale, myself, and Jerry's manager Larry Spellman, we wondered where Don disappeared for a minute or two. He was in the dressing room having a cigarette. Everyone chided him, but he just smiled weakly.

Iris Cornell intends to carry on Don's great legacy of music: "Which we will have forever and ever."

Some of Don Cornell's Italian recordings are "Forget Domani," "Andiamo," "Mala Femmena," "Al-Di-La," "Non Dimenticar," "Ciao, Ciao Bambina," "Innamorata," "Come Back to Sorrento," "Volare," "Arrivederci, Roma," and are represented best on his *Something to Remember Me By*, Vol. I and II and *I'll Be Seeing You* Vol I and II albums currently available.

Al Monroe's Eulogy to Don Cornell on February 26, 2004 at the Riverside Gordon Memorial Chapel in Aventura, Florida

Ladies and Gentleman.

I truly believe the good Lord was looking after me by making it possible for me to be in Florida at this trying time to say farewell to my cherished friend, Don Cornell. Don was 84, going on 85 this April and, may I say: "It Isn't Fair." As you know, people now-a-days live into their 90s and beyond.

Of course, we all know Don for his legendary career as a singer, entertainer, and for his endless list of hit recordings. Fortunately for us, Don was performing up until a little less than a year ago and, as I reminded him, he still sounded as great as he did back in those 1950s recording studios when he made all those great records. In fact, Don was the very last of the big band singers to be performing. On stage, Don was very special with that great voice and charming charisma. He possessed a big, booming voice that was touched with beautiful shadings which resulted in each of Don's songs finding their way into the hearts of his loving fans everywhere. Don was a man filled with compassion, warmth, humor, integrity, kindness, and generosity, so I am indeed extremely proud to say that Don Cornell was a cherished friend. Just to have known him will always make me feel special. Don's love for his wife, Iris, ran very deep. Each Don Cornell performance concluded with Don singing "The Wind Beneath My Wings," as a tribute to Iris, who was wonderfully loving, helpful and unselfish. Don has gone up to the big concert hall in the sky, but always remember, besides the great memories we each have of him, he left us a legacy of great recordings, which the entire world will have to enjoy forever and ever. God Bless Don Cornell, and I still say "It Isn't Fair."

Loving words from Iris Cornell

"Losing Don was overwhelming for me, as I shared twenty-five wonderful years with this beautiful, kind and gentle man. He was special in so many ways and he made me feel special in return, not only by being a loving husband, but by allowing me the privilege of being his helpmate during his long and great musical career. It give me great comfort knowing how adored he was by his family, his many friends, and the fans that followed his career for more than fifty years. They too were heartbroken when they heard of Don's passing. Don was the last of the Big Band singers. That musical era is now gone, but Don's wonderful and unmistakable voice will live on through his so many recordings. Music has lost it's best friend. I know I have. 'It Isn't Fair.'"

I'll Be Seeing You...

VOL I	VOL II
That Old Feeling	Let A Smile Be Your Umbrella
Was That The Human Thing To Do?	When I Take My Sugar To Tea
I Have But One Heart	Volare
Stay As Sweet As You Are	Danger! Heartbreak Ahead
S'posin'	Unchained Melody
Are You Lonesome Tonight?	Return To Me
You're Breaking My Heart	Baby, It's Cold Outside
All Of You	That's The Chance You Take
Forget About Me	Wedding Bells (That Old Gang Of Mine)
We Three (My Echo, My Shadow and Me)	Most Of All
Flying Trapeze	Innamorata
My Mother's Pearls	Free To Love You
I	I've Only Myself To Blame
Rock Island Line	Arrivederci, Roma
Many Are The Times	Size 12
Just Say I Love Her	A Cottage For Sale
You'll Never Get Away	The Breeze
I Need You So	You Call It Madness, But I Call It Love
Come Back To Sorrento	Please Play Our Song (Mr. Record Man)
But Not Your Heart	You Know You Don't Want Me
The Bible Tells Me So	I Think I'll Fall In Love Today
When I Was A Child	Pretend You Don't See Her
Let's Have An Old Fashioned Christmas	I'll Be Seeing You

RETURN TO ME

(RITORNAA ME)

Words and Music by CARMEN LOMBARDO and DANNY DI MINNO

as Recorded by
DEAN MARTIN
on CAPITOL RECORDS

Sole Selling Agent:

SOUTHERN MUSIC PUB. CO., INC. 1619 BROADWAY, NEW YORK 19, N. Y.

Dino Crocetti

Dean Martin

For Dean Martin Nothing was Ever A Big Deal...Especially Fame.

When I was a young man working as a studio page at NBC in New York, I volunteered on the very first Dean Martin and Jerry Lewis Telethon in studio 6B on March 15, 1952. My job was greeting and logging in the talent and recording their time in and out. Many great celebrities performed for charity that historic 24 hours including Nat King Cole, Jackie Gleason, Ezio Pinza, Yul Brynner, Mel Torme, Ella Fitzgerald, Frank Sinatra, Milton Berle, Eddie Fisher [in his U.S. Army uniform], Perry Como, Cab Calloway - the list goes on. I recall Dean being a very casual but polished performer, always gracious and grateful to his guests for appearing with him and Jerry for their favorite charity. At the time, Dean Martin and Jerry Lewis were securely anchored within 'big time' show business.

And, I learned a lot about Dean Martin from Lee Hale, a fellow member of the Society of Singers, who was associated with Dean for nine years on *The Dean Martin Television Show,* both as musical director and rehearsal stand-in for Dean. Lee was once a singer himself, appearing with a singing group named the Manhattans. He was also choral director for *The Bell Telephone Hour* and *The Entertainers* television shows. Lee produced NBC's historical *The First Fifty Years* that earned four Emmy nominations. Lee personally earned two: one for producing and one for video editing. He has been musical director for shows starring Bob Hope, Gene Kelly, Bob Newhart, Dinah Shore, Lena Horne, Peggy Lee, Tony Bennett, Jimmy Stewart, and Jonathan Winters. But, Lee, who was very close to Dean Martin for all the years the show ran, and who is the author of "Backstage with the Dean Martin Show" (written with his friend, Richard Neely,) recounts the professional part of Dean's story best, and in Lee's own words.

Lee Hale

Dean Martin was unique, one of a kind. Tall, dark and handsome. Dean was a man's man and a lady's desire, and could sing as well as any singer of his day. According to every comedian he ever worked with, including former partner Jerry Lewis, Dean was the world's best straight man.

Dean Martin hit the big time when he teamed up with Jerry Lewis while performing in East coast night clubs during the mid-1940s.

"I was supposed to be the singing half and Jerry the comic," Dean said," and we both did a lot of both."

(R. Grudens Collection)

The boys began their ascent in show business. Their routines were almost always ad-libs. The onstage antics had audiences howling. Fans began to expect the unexpected. Soon they completed a flock of hit movies for Paramount, and their appearances on NBC's Colgate Comedy Hour pushed them to the top of the coveted Neilson ratings.

Through all this, Dean was the anything goes kinda guy, while Jerry wanted to take charge, even produce, consequently reducing Dean's responsibilities. One day, and for no particular reason Dean could remember, the easy going Italian Crooner simply walked away.

"Everybody thought that was a big mistake on my part," Dean said, "after all, Jerry was supposed to be the funny one and I was just the straight man." Afterwards, Dean sashayed his way through a couple of forgettable MGM movies. It seemed the public assumed his career was over. But Dean knew better. Booked as a solo act in the best Las Vegas showrooms, he found a prop that would establish his image from then on: a glass of scotch liquor. Vegas audiences, both male and female, found him lovable. "I was just one of the guys," he would always say. That glass of scotch was mostly water.

Lee Hale and His Boss Watching the Monitor
(Lee Hale Collection)

Some accused him of being a drunk, but Dean always replied, "I would remind those people that I couldn't possibly do all the things I was doing if I were soused." Concluding, NBC would not pay him millions if he were a drunk. They would've canceled the show if he showed up drunk even once, no matter how big a star he would be. There was only apple juice in that glass. I know. I was there.

Some funny guest spots on a couple of TV specials led NBC to offer him a weekly hour of his own. It was the time, you know, when variety shows were the staple of prime time television. But Dean wasn't sure he'd like fronting a weekly show. Many of his co-performers had tried and failed (including Jerry), and besides, "Why would I want to waste six or seven days a week rehearsing. I had better things to do - like play golf - watch the soaps, or maybe a movie or two," Dean pointed out. So he told NBC they could have him only if he didn't have to rehearse all week and if he could come in just one day a week, and that day had to be Sunday; and if they would pay him a lot of money.

To his total surprise, NBC said, "Yes!" There was trouble at first. The bookings were fashioned around circus type acts and Dean played Ed Sullivan: "And now, I'd like to present..."

Then maybe he'd sing a chorus of "That's Amore," "Pennies From Heaven" or "Memories are Made of This," depending on how he felt that day. After the first show, he performed with a multitude of pals including Frank Sinatra and Diahann Carroll, the ratings plummeted. The show's producer was fired and its director, Greg Garrison, assumed both jobs. With ideas on how to boost the ratings, he hired me as a special material writer and musical director. We had to find a way to use Dean more and keep the one-day-a-week schedule.

I loved working with Dean Martin. We got along just fine. I figured out ways to work in little routines with guests, and Greg stopped booking trained seals and trapeze acts. He brought in comedians, singers, movie stars and TV performers who seldom did variety shows. And, there were the girls - the Golddiggers, every one a beauty. I would carefully rehearse the guests all week long, explaining they would have just one chance with him at the taping where we would be charming, gracious, and surprisingly easy to work with. Sometimes panic set in a guest the first time, but they usually returned in later appearances knowing exactly what to expect, happily going along with the unusual procedure.

It was discovered that the less Dean knew about the show, the more it became spontaneous and funny. Greg always kept the tape rolling, even the goofs, because Dean made his mistakes appear to be well-rehearsed. His experience with Jerry gave him an endless supply of one-liners and stock routines that could endlessly get him out of any awkward situation.

With Dean's easy-going manner and his fine singing voice, the ratings began to rise. Our experiment worked. Dean would arrive around noon Sunday for a snappy music run through with Les Brown and his band. In his dressing room Dean would watch Greg and I go through his sketches and songs on a television monitor. Later, the audience filed into Burbank Studio # 4 and the taping began. It took an hour to tape the show. Before the band finished playing the closing theme, our star was out of the studio and into his sports car.

Sure, Dean Martin was a major star, a wonderful singer, and a great nightclub entertainer, but, to me, it was his TV show that revealed the *real* Dean Martin. What you saw in your living room was exactly the kind of guy he actually was: entirely likable, with a terrific sense of humor, simply a perfect performer. Nobody will ever do what he did: pop in and do an hour's show without rehearsal and make it so entertaining.

For nine long years, Dean Martin never balked at anything we threw at him - and sometimes those things were outrageous. Remember the time we had him him slide down a pole and go straight through the floor, or when he leaped up on his piano and it collapsed under him? Dean made my job easy. No matter what song we gave him, or what surprise guest appeared, he always performed with enthusiasm and excellence.

Oh, Yes! I remember that Dean Martin personally chose his one ballad performed in the middle of the show - you know, the one he'd sing with Ken Lane at the piano. You may remember those ubiquitous cue cards on which he greatly depended, or the girls pushing him this way or that. Dean would stare at me offstage as I cued his entrances. Every time he came out on the studio stage, he'd look around for me, "I owe my life to you out there," he once confided to me. His struggles with the cue cards added charm to the show.

What great fun we had, and what I'd give to bring back those glorious days. I sure miss my friend Dean Martin, one of the best Italian Crooners ever.

Back in 1998, while waiting to interview Jerry Vale backstage at the Westbury Music Fair on Long Island, I ran smack into one of Dean Martin's most popular and frequent guests, comedian Dom DeLuise. I sequestered him into one of the prop rooms adjoining his dressing room and he recalled for me the Dean Martin he knew and loved.

"I love working with Dom De Luise. Such a funny, funny talented man. No one is better!." Dean Martin.

Dom De Luise

I was very nervous when I first appeared on Dean's show. He was an established star and I was very young and frightened. Producer Greg Garrison took me into Dean's dressing room. Dean was very sweet - he gave me a kiss and a hug - and was very kind to me. I was on and off his show for nine years, and later on the roasts shows. Dean was very spontaneous, and he really didn't care what anybody expected him to do, so we would rehearse with Lee Hale doing Dean's part - Lee was in charge of all the music on the show and he would do it, but in a dry, but adequate way. Dean would invariably watch it

Richard and Dom, 1999 backstage at Westbury (B. Debetta Photo)

- then do it, having come in only on the day of the show's taping. Big stars like Peter Sellers, Mickey Rooney, Jack Benny, Jimmy Stewart, and Kate Smith would work all week long. "When is Dean coming?" was always the question.

In one sketch Dean was trying to mate his parakeet. The first line was - and I would say, "How do you do?" - then Lee - behaving like Dean - would say, "How do you do?" But when Dean came in front of the audience, I would say," How do you do?" and Dean answered, "How do you do *what*?" So the show was spontaneous even though we had rehearsed it. Dean, however, was doing it for the first time. I remember Dean being pushed along this way and that way on his own show - by the girls who knew where he was supposed to be standing, or he looked offstage to Lee Hale - and was even pushed in one direction or another by one of the guests who knew where Dean was to move to. He laughed and loved it while we were taping, and they kept it in. People loved it.

But, Dean was a family man, his children would come to visit him all the time, and, if you were sick, he would always call you. When Dean lost his son, that was very sad because we all felt for him so. (Dean's son, Dean Paul Martin, was killed in 1987 when a jet fighter he was piloting on military maneuvers crashed.)

There was a two week period where Dean didn't perform, and then he went to Vegas. The audience knew he'd been through this tragedy, and when he came out, they cheered and applauded. I saw him weep that night - and he started his routine and he was hysterically funny and sang so well. At the end they gave him another ovation and he cried again - and that was the reentry from that tragedy back into show business for Dean Martin. He was sweet - without another agenda. He was always right there for you. He always complimented me - on how funny I was - and that was great. I once watched Dean sing a song and I was very impressed. I went over to him and said, "Dean, that was great!" Now I had known Dean for ten years - and I don't know how many times I complimented him - and he said, "Really! Was it that good?" And, I thought, Oh, my God! Here's Dean Martin - this big, big star and he is cherishing my compliment - which I really meant with all my heart, but I couldn't believe he needed it like I always need it. He was genuinely touched. And that's great to see that part of him. It was a gift from God to have worked with him and to have known him. I still miss Dean Martin.

LOOKING BACK OVER MY SHOULDER

Dean was born Dino Crocetti in Steubenville, Ohio, on June 7, 1917. His father, Guy Crochetti, owned a barber shop. Dean would sing at picnics and local dance halls and was occasionally mixed up in a little mischief now and then. He also tried honest work in that limited steel community, shining shoes, pumping gas, boxing (until he broke his nose), and as a blackjack dealer in one of the city's gambling operations, being a fast guy with a deck of cards.

Dino, as he was known, enjoyed listening to Bing Crosby's recordings and thought he too could sing in that laid back kind of style if he tried. He began singing in bars and clubs run by friends where he learned to handle and ply an audience. In 1939, he joined up with Ernie McKay's band. Ernie altered Dino's name to Dino Martini. His pay? Forty dollars a week. He later joined Sammy Watkins band in Cleveland, that led to a four year contract. It was Sammy who suggested the stage name of Dean Martin.

One night Dean found himself looking into the pretty eyes of Betty McDonald. They began dating, married and had a baby. The little family moved to New York where Dean was engaged as a replacement for Frank Sinatra, but did not do as well as Frank had, abruptly ending that gig. He shuttled from contract to contract, finally sending Betty and their now two children back home while he remained to find new work. He teamed up, as singers did in those days, with a comic or other act, and one day in New York was booked with a kid named Joey Levitch, the son of a husband and wife vaudeville team. He called himself Jerry Lewis. After the engagement they went their separate ways only to run into one another a year later, in 1945.

Jerry was having a hard time staying on the bill where he was booked to perform his single comedy act. He talked to Dean's agent about following Dean with antics: When Dean was singing, Jerry, dressed as a waiter, dropped a tray of dishes. Jerry would ad-lib and perform antics that would include working the audience. They did pretty well. Jerry suggested they team up, but Dean decided against it, preferring his own independence.

Soon they were both out of work. However, Jerry had a booking at The 500 Club in Atlantic City, but bombed out. He placed a hasty call to Dean's agent in New York and begged Dean to join him. The agent worked a deal for both of them to perform as a single act. It worked: As Dean attempted to sing, Jerry, as the inept waiter, dropped drinks and dishes off his tray. Taunting Dean and throwing steaks at him, taking over the drums in the band, drowning out Dean's songs, spritzing him with seltzer water, and creating havoc, almost destroying the club, Dean would laugh, but continued singing as Jerry romped through his hijinks. Before long, now in demand, the pair rocked New York nightclubs and prevailed as the hottest act of 1948. All this was followed by television appearances on the *Ed Sullivan Show* and *Texaco Star Theater* and engagements in Los Angeles and Miami. By this time Betty (with their now three kids) filed for divorce, as a normal life for her and Dean became impossible since he was never home. Dean soon met Jeannie Biegger, a pretty blonde model, while performing in Miami and married her a month after his divorce from Betty became final.

After a few movies and a milk-warm try at an NBC radio show of their own, the pair garnered a coveted, regular spot as rotating guests on the *Colgate Comedy Hour* television show and simultaneously signed with top-rated agency, MCA, to manage their contract bookings and financial affairs. They sprinted through 16 films between 1949 and 1956 and appeared in person for the last time in 1956 at the Copacabana New York. Over time, Dean felt exploited by Jerry, who dominated their professional relationship and diminished Dean's contributions to the act.

Many insiders figured that Dean Martin would not make it on his own without the presence of Jerry Lewis. However, as you know, after a slow start, which began in Las Vegas, Dean was immensely successful with his nine yearlong television show and went on to make over thirty additional films without Jerry Lewis, and costarred with John Wayne, Frank Sinatra, and Bing Crosby. His pivotal role in *The Young Lions* in 1958, *Rio Bravo* in 1959, and the *Sons of Katie Elder* in 1965 were straight dramatic performances, devoid of any singing or comedy and he held his own quite nicely. Dean spoofed through a couple of Matt Helm private eye films in the 1960s.

Appearing in the film, Budd Shulberg's *Some Came Running* with his future blood brother, and fellow Italian Crooner, Frank Sinatra, helped establish the famous "Rat Pack" composed of Frank, Dean, Sammy Davis, Jr., comedian Joey Bishop and British actor Peter Lawford.

Dean joined Frank Sinatra at Frank's Reprise Records where he recorded "Everybody Loves Somebody" suggested and written by his future piano accompaniest Ken Lane.

Ironically, Dean's success on a *Hollywood Palace* television show was a replacement for the ailing two-hour ABC *Jerry Lewis Show*. The *Palace* led to the NBC series *The Dean Martin Show* that ran for nine years, followed by Friar Club Television Roasts, Vegas dates, movies, TV specials, and lots of golf...Yes! Golf. Romance followed romance. Jeannie divorced Dean in 1972. Dean tried marriage once more with Kathy Hawn.

A memorable event occurred on Jerry Lewis' 1976 Muscular Dystrophy Telethon. Frank Sinatra came on and sang his songs, and then informed Jerry he had a friend that, well "...loves what you do every year and would like to come out." Upon that declaration, Dean Martin meandered out and embraced Jerry Lewis. It had been twenty years. It was an emotional and genuine greeting. Jerry chirped," Ya working?" that broke up everyone. Dean sang with Frank and blew Jerry a final kiss and left. The audience was enthralled. Jerry was enthralled.

On a last ditched, final tour with Frank and Sammy, Dean bolted, flew back home and checked into a hospital. Liza Minelli took Dean's spot for the tour's remainder. Dean's health deteriorated over a short period and Jeannie returned to his side. His voice became weak. His spirit diminished.

Of Dean's best singing hit records, "Everybody Loves Somebody," "That's Amore," from the 1953 film with Jerry entitled *The Caddy*, "Memories Are Made of This," and "Return to Me," may be remembered as his most popular recordings.

We lost the voice, the laugh, and the charm of Dean Martin on Christmas Day, 1995.

In 1998 John Chintala completed a 450 page book entitled *Dean Martin-A Complete Guide to the Total Entertainer*. This very valid reference book documents the complete achievements of Dean Martin in motion pictures, radio, television, and recordings. John has written for many publications that include DISCoveries and Filmfax, and has contributed to *American Movie Classics - Coming Attractions* television programs.

According to John, Dean recorded over 600 songs, hosted 275 Dean Martin television shows and performed as a guest on 200 more. Dean starred in 50 films and performed on over 100 radio shows and sang during countless nightclub appearances. "The notion that Dean Martin 'coasted' through his career is completely exaggerated." That was just the face he showed the world.

"Dean paid great homage to his ancestry on his album *Italian Love Songs* album," John added," so Dean rightfully belongs in this book about all his Italian counterparts like Perry Como, Jimmy Roselli, Frank Sinatra, Jerry Vale, Al Martino, and Tony Bennett.

"And, while you are looking through my own or this very book, play one of Dean's albums and listen to his voice glide effortlessly through 'This Time I'm Swingin,' " or one of his charming Italian tunes like 'That's Amore,' and maybe, - just maybe, you'll forget your troubles 'cause Dino is singing, pally, and all is right with the world."

THE BREEZE AND I

Lyric by AL STILLMAN   Music by ERNESTO LECUONA

Adapted By T. CAMARATA *From* ERNESTO LECUONA'S

"ANDALUCIA"

Recorded by
VIC DAMONE

RECORDED ON:
Capitol—Billy May
Mercury—Vic Damone
MASTERTOUCH AND BROADWAY ROLLS

INCLUDING
SHEFTE
PIANO SOLO

3/-

J. ALBERT & SON PTY LTD
MUSIC PUBLISHERS
SYDNEY   WELLINGTON, N.Z.
MELBOURNE
EDWARD B. MARKS MUSIC CORP., NEW YORK
AUTHORISED FOR SALE ONLY IN AUSTRALIA AND NEW ZEALAND

Vito Rocco Farinola

Vic Damone

"The Best Set of Pipes in the Business." *Frank Sinatra*

In 1997 Vic Damone (Damone, his mom's maiden name) celebrated 50 years in the singing business and performed to a sold-out, one-man Carnegie Hall concert on January 24, 1998. Backed by a 40 piece orchestra, the sixty-nine year old sang like a man half his age. He performed three great standards, Mitchell Parish and Heinz Roemheld's "Ruby" (which he does so well), Hammerstein and Kern's "The Song is You," and Brooks Bowman's "East of the Sun." After the performance ended, his very excited publicist Rob Wilcox told me:

"... the show was a terrific success for Damone, beyond his wildest dreams."

Before it all came to fruition for Vic Damone, who was born in Brooklyn on June 12, 1928, he had emerged on the scene in the late 1940s, never serving an apprenticeship with the big bands like Bing Crosby, Frank Sinatra, or Don Cornell did before him, Vic had worked as an usher at the New York Paramount and became influenced by Frank Sinatra, having worked when Sinatra was performing there. Vic won an *Arthur Godfrey Talent Show* contest in 1943 singing "Prisoner of Love," a song made famous by Russ Columbo, Bing Crosby, and later, Perry Como, too.

Vic's recording career took off when he signed with Mercury Records after having spent a short spell with Silvertone Records. He had his own CBS radio show in 1947 and 1948. With Mercury he recorded Lionel Newman's "Again" from the 1948 film *Roadhouse*, and "You're Breaking My Heart," which first attracted me to his career. Both recordings remain important evergreens.

BANDLEADER BEN GRISAFI

"Vic and I attended Lafayette High School together when he was Vito Farinola and lived on 86th street. We dated the same girl, Jean Creco, and he

took her to St. Finbar's Catholic Church Confraternity dance on Bath Avenue, Brooklyn where I was playing there with the Marty Alma Big Band. I later played for Vic's sister's wedding at the Casa Del Rey Caterer's on Coney Island Avenue. He was not able to attend because he was filming in LA, but sent a telegram which he asked me to read aloud to the newlyweds. He sang great in those days and he still sings great today. We renewed our friendship now and then over the years, once after his Carnegie Hall appearance and then at Las Vegas, where he was performing. Interesting to say, Vic always wore a turtle neck sweater from his earliest days 'til today believing it protected his throat - thus saving his voice."

Vic's early voicing was similar in style to Sinatra, especially on a 1946 radio air check "You Go to My Head," and "All Through the Day," performed live on radio station WHN in New York.

"Most songs had been recorded by Frank," Vic said, "but you have to try to present a new interpretation. You want to be your own man." Vic cheerfully admits the emulation was deliberate at the time. "I tried to mimic him. My training and learning process was watching all those performers on stage. I decided that if I could *sound* like Frank, maybe I did have a chance after all."

For me, Vic Damone's most appealing recording was Pat Genaro and Sunny Skylar's "You're Breaking My Heart," which will always be his best just as Tony Bennett's is "I Left My Heart in San Francisco." Vic, of course, never sang with the bands, but he appeared in a movie, *The Strip*, with big band greats Louis Armstrong, Jack Teagarden and pianist Earl Hines. In the 1955 film *Hit the Deck*, Vic performed Vincent Youmans' joyous "Sometimes I'm Happy," and it was arranger/conductor Frank De Vol who directed him singing a now Damone signature tune "An Affair to Remember," the title song from the 1957 hit movie of the same name.

In his later works, Vic seemed to avoid the old standards, but always sings Lerner and Loewe's classic "On the Street Where You Live" from the Broadway musical *My Fair Lady,* for my money the definitive version of that song.

In 1966, Vic toured with Bob Hope's USO troupe at Chu Lai, Vietnam. When they were up in a plane as they approached Pleiku, home of the 4th Infantry Division, Vic asked Bob," What are those puffs of smoke down there? Artillery fire?" And Bob replied," No, they're just burning General Charles De Gaulle's photograph."

Vic Damone kinda retired for a while, then appeared back on the scene in the early eighties, mostly because of a renaissance he enjoyed in England. It seems that a DJ, BBC's David Jacob's, gave Vic a lot of airplay, heavily featuring Vic's 1961 album *The Pleasure of Her Company*, from a Fred Astaire musical comedy film. Vic had toured the British Isles to standing room audiences during the eighties.

"When he walked on stage, before he sung a note, he received a standing ovation every time, everywhere," said Denis Brown in a newsletter of the Dick Haymes Society. In 1996, twenty-five of Vic's Mercury Recordings were reissued under the title *The Mercury Years*.

After his marriage to Diahann Carroll in 1987, they joined forces and made appearances as a team at all the renown venues.

127

This was the fourth marriage for each. After a while, bookers would expect Vic to always appear with Diahann, which distracted and limited his engagements after their separation.

Vic appeared onstage as Sky Masterson at Westbury Music Fair in a revival of the 1940s Broadway musical production *Guys and Dolls*. Over the years he has performed regularly at Michael's Pub and Rainbow & Stars in New York, and in important engagements in Las Vegas and Atlantic City.

It is said that Vic Damone doesn't really enjoy the *business* of show business, "But, I'm never tired of singing," he says emphatically. Lucky for Vic Damone, Reader's Digest had issued *The Legendary Vic Damone*, album, an excellent quality 3-CD set with 30 new and 30 old Capitol Damone evergreens. The combination of four Damone songs with the great arranger and conductor Nelson Riddle, and a ten tune "live" group from his 1963 engagement at Basin Street East, coupled with Broadway and Hollywood tracks, are truly worth owning.

In 1995, appearing at Rainbow & Stars in New York's Rockefeller Center with an entirely new show entitled *An Affair to Remember,* Vic's crooning still sent them swooning, according to a Cabaret Review in the N.Y. News:

"Looking ever so cool, he moves with the music, snapping his fingers, bobbing his head and titling his shoulders. Savoring each syllable, he sings in a rich, conversational baritone that's still robust and romantic." A true Italian troubadour.

"I guess I have had it all. A great career, marriage, divorce, have a son, daughters, more wives, all these trials and tribulations, joys and hurts, then I had a life, and I began to use everything I learned in my singing, even learning how to box, which taught me, someone who grew up with four sisters, about the physical side of life. The only thing I regret is that I never got to go through the trials and tribulations of being a singer before I was completely scrutinized. I missed that process. Sinatra had a couple of years of singing around in clubs before it happened to him."

Nice thing about Vic, he always talks to fans, even after exhausting performances.

Vic's "Farewell Performance" on February 10, 2001 at the Kravit's Center in West Palm Beach, Florida, backed by a 60 piece orchestra, was a night to remember for him and so many of his fans. It followed a mild stroke, and his wife Rena Rowan-Damone, through her special care, helped bring him up to this farewell show. Attending was his four children, son Perry (a Phoenix, Arizona radio show host), and daughters Victoria, Andrea, and Daniella, and his grandchildren. Rena, formerly chief fashion designer at *Jones New York,* heads several philanthropic foundations to help various charities.

Lately, when appearing here or there, Vic has casually talked about reviving his career. We will have to keep tuned to find out if it's true.

The Movies

1951 *Rich, Young and Pretty* with Jane Powell.
1951 *The Strip* with Mickey Rooney, and Louis Armstrong and Jack Teagarden as themselves.
1954 *The Girl Next Door* with Jane Powell.
1954 *Athena* - as Johnny Nyle
1954 *Deep in My Heart* a cameo in a biography of composer Sigmund Romberg
1955 *Hit the Deck,* as Rico Ferrari
1955 *Kismet*, As the Caliph
1957 *An Affair to Remember* - the singing voice of film title.
1958 *Separate Tables* - Where he sang the title song.
1958 *War and Peace* - Sang title song; and countless radio and television appearances .

SPANISH EYES

Music by BERT KAEMPFERT

Lyrics by CHARLES SINGLETON and EDDIE SNYDER

04549

Recorded by AL MARTINO on CAPITOL RECORDS

Roosevelt Music Co., Inc.

75¢

Alfred Cino

Al Martino

Al Martino and I go back to 1998 when we talked about his wondrous career as a class "A" singer of all the great ballads, Italian and otherwise. And, he's from Philadelphia like our newer singer friends John Primerano and Lou Lanza.

Al, formerly Alfred Cino, croons those great tunes "Here in My Heart," "I Love You More and More Each Day," "Mary In the Morning," and his signature classic, the million seller and overwhelming international favorite, "Spanish Eyes," that melts the hearts of his faithful.

Al's Italian immigrant dad was a brick layer and builder of postwar homes. Al first worked with him in the construction of the homes. An older friend, the legendary Mario Lanza, encouraged Al to pursue his own career as a singer.

"As an impressionable youngster, I got started the same way so many others did, I listened and was influenced by other singers on the radio. There was Al Jolson, Tony Martin, Sinatra, Perry Como, Frankie Laine - and so I bought their records and began to sing along with them. Of course, you haven't developed your own style yet - it doesn't appear until years later."

Talking to Al Martino that day from his Beverly Hills home, we touched on the development of his singing style: "I began to vocalize first with a piano, then with a trio at local clubs around Philadelphia, and then I became a winner on an *Arthur Godfrey's Talent Scouts* show, and before you knew it, I was making records." Knowing he had to go to New York, Al did just that and made the rounds of music companies.

Luckily for Al, he found a backer right away in Bill Borrelli, who had heard him on the talent show. "He liked the way I sang and thought I would be the perfect singer to record a song he was working on called 'Here in My Heart,' Al recalled, "So with two other financial backers, Busillo and Smith, we formed the recording company BBS Records, perhaps the very first independent record label, just to produce my first recording." It was, of course, the first time that very popular song was ever sung or recorded. And, like a miracle, it went straight to number one on the charts.

"We had no idea it would score that well, even though I liked the song very much from the beginning, and it was actually written just for me."

Monty Kelly, an arranger and friend of Al Martino, worked diligently with him, locating and rehearsing quality studio musicians, directing the orchestra in the careful arrangement of this recording. "When you want to make a record, you simply hire an orchestra. That's the usual pattern. You don't have to have your own established orchestra to make a record, "Al explained.

R. Grudens Collection

Al brought the newly-produced recording to Johnny Mercer's Capitol Records: "I drove to California in my Father's 1952 Ford taking the record with the BBS label - it took me three days to get there - and tried to sell it to Capitol. I had but five days to seal the deal, as I had made an agreement in Philadelphia that if I didn't sell the record to Capitol within five days, it would revert back to another manufacturer owned by Dave Miller. I had to forfeit all my royalties if Capitol didn't buy it. That was the gamble. As bad luck would have it, they didn't. So I gave it to Mr. Miller. It became a hit, as we all now know, and, of course, I received no royalties."

"Nothing at all?" I asked. "Not one penny."

I reminded Al that Patty Andrews and her sisters received only fifty dollars for recording "Bie Mir Bist Du Schoen, "and had to split it three ways.

"I know too that Fran Warren received but fifty dollars for her classic hit recording "Sunday Kind of Love" made with Claude Thornhill's orchestra," Al recalled.

It happened to so many singers during those early recording days according to both Connie Haines and Jo Stafford, told to me during interviews.

Another very memorable Al Martino vignette:

"In the early sixties I heard an instrumental melody on the radio called 'Moon Over Naples,' which was written by German orchestra leader and composer Bert Keampfert. It had been released in America, and I had a copy of it, but I didn't know there were lyrics written to it.

Then somebody wrote a lyric, I heard it on the radio, and I didn't like it at all. So I called the published and said, 'If you dump that record that's out there right now, I'll give you an exclusive on a new and much better lyric.' I had alternate lyrics written for the song by Ted Snider and Larry McCousick."

That event happened in 1965. It became Al Martino's biggest hit and one of the most popular records of all time. The song: "Spanish Eyes."

As Al's career took hold, he did very well singing in and for the movies. He performed "Hush, Hush, Sweet Charlotte" for the Bette Davis film of the same name, which led to the coveted role of Johnny Fontane in the 1972 award-winning film *The Godfather.* The

tune was an Italian piece entitled "O Marenariello" ("I Have But One Heart,") written by Johnny Farrow. It was perfectly suited for Al. He also recorded the film's poignant theme "Speak Softly, Love."
"Phyllis McGuire of the McGuire sisters called me to say she read the book. She knew about my life more than any other performer so she thought I was perfect for the part. I was, like other singers who sang in nightclubs, employed by organized crime in the beginning. So I had my own story that paralleled the character of Johnny Fontaine. The director, Francis Ford Coppola didn't want me in the film for some obscure reason, so I had to reach some pretty

important people over his head to remain in the film. I didn't enjoy working on a film knowing the director didn't want me, and that's why I turned down the next *Godfather* film. I was pretty busy at the time and didn't care to work with him."

Al Martino declares he has no personal favorites among his recordings: "I consider all my songs equal

Band Leader Ben Grisafi and Al Martino

to one another. 'I Love You More and More Every Day,' 'Here in My Heart,' 'I Love You Because,' 'Spanish Eyes,' 'Volare', and the Italian song 'To the Door of the Sun,' all the songs that people still play every day - songs that became Top Ten hits like 'Mary in the Morning.' That's a kinda folk song, and the others, you know, are also great songs. I feel the same way about all the singers I know, too. I love and enjoy them all. I really do."

Al doesn't vocalize much when he is at home, except when rehearsing, which he does while playing piano. "That's the only way I can keep my voice in shape all the time...it keeps me going." Al maintains that he sings much better today than he did yesterday. Many recent reviews back that fact. " ...as the old story goes, if I only knew then what I know today...of course I sing much better today. I have more knowledge and experience, and I've learned how to use my voice best."

"It's not always easy selecting a song you want to record. For me, the best way to hear a song is to get a good demo of it...especially from the composer. He usually will send you a lead sheet set for the piano, but that's not good enough. You have to have the writer's interpretation, because he wrote it. Johnny Symbol wrote 'Mary In the Morning' and sent me a demo of him singing it while he played the guitar. So I hired him to play at the recording session."

That song is one of Al Martino's most popular and the one he still receives so many requests for at concerts. Like so many American vocalists, Al Martino's recordings fare better in Europe. "People in Europe are true music lovers. Here, they mostly think of just one thing - rock and roll, or rap, or anything dished up and pushed upon the public by Top 40 radio. In Europe, especially the adults, they appreciate our kind of music and promote and play it consistently over the rock stuff."

Al lived in England from 1953 to 1959 where he enjoyed a great popularity as a performer. While trying to get a hold of him for updated material for this book, I found he was performing in Germany, where he frequently tours. From Germany he flies back to his home in California and back again to the East coast where he did a one night, annual show, at Westbury Music Fair, where I finally caught up with him.

About possible retirement: "I believe in being productive. That's why I will never retire. It's not a question of how long I can go. I think one should always be productive. Retirement is out of the question because it means you are unproductive. What am I trying to prove? This! If a person wants to be productive - survive - he has no alternative. He has to keep going. I think I have reached that point now. I'm supposed to be productive, and I am. I love performing on the *road*. I love to record. I also *love* to ski. It's what you want to do. It's called *living*. I like to *work* and *live*."

Al Martino personally appeared during a pledge week promotion, on August 8, 2004, on Public Television, wherein they presented a one hour concert he made during the 1970s in Edmonton, Canada, performing his almost entire book of songs. Interviewed awkwardly by WLIWs Mark Simone, Al talked

WORDS — HONEY COME BACK WHATEVER HAPPENED (BABY) TO YOU AND I		WORDS — HONEY COME BACK WHATEVER HAPPENED (BABY) TO YOU AND I	
STEREO **AL MARTINO** Capitol LP Album — CAN'T HELP FALLING IN LOVE STEREO	STEREO	**AL MARTINO** Capitol LP Album — CAN'T HELP FALLING IN LOVE	STEREO
SWEET CAROLINE — MY WAY YOU'RE ALL THE WOMAN THAT I NEED		SWEET CAROLINE — MY WAY YOU'RE ALL THE WOMAN THAT I NEED	
WORDS — HONEY COME BACK WHATEVER HAPPENED (BABY) TO YOU AND I		WORDS — HONEY COME BACK WHATEVER HAPPENED (BABY) TO YOU AND I	
STEREO **AL MARTINO** Capitol LP Album — CAN'T HELP FALLING IN LOVE STEREO	STEREO	**AL MARTINO** Capitol LP Album — CAN'T HELP FALLING IN LOVE	STEREO
SWEET CAROLINE — MY WAY YOU'RE ALL THE WOMAN THAT I NEED		SWEET CAROLINE — MY WAY YOU'RE ALL THE WOMAN THAT I NEED	
WORDS — HONEY COME BACK WHATEVER HAPPENED (BABY) TO YOU AND I		WORDS — HONEY COME BACK WHATEVER HAPPENED (BABY) TO YOU AND I	
STEREO **AL MARTINO** Capitol LP Album — CAN'T HELP FALLING IN LOVE STEREO	STEREO	**AL MARTINO** Capitol LP Album — CAN'T HELP FALLING IN LOVE	STEREO
SWEET CAROLINE — MY WAY YOU'RE ALL THE WOMAN THAT I NEED		SWEET CAROLINE — MY WAY YOU'RE ALL THE WOMAN THAT I NEED	
WORDS — HONEY COME BACK WHATEVER HAPPENED (BABY) TO YOU AND I		WORDS — HONEY COME BACK WHATEVER HAPPENED (BABY) TO YOU AND I	
STEREO **AL MARTINO** Capitol LP Album — CAN'T HELP FALLING IN LOVE STEREO	STEREO	**AL MARTINO** Capitol LP Album — CAN'T HELP FALLING IN LOVE	STEREO
SWEET CAROLINE — MY WAY YOU'RE ALL THE WOMAN THAT I NEED		SWEET CAROLINE — MY WAY YOU'RE ALL THE WOMAN THAT I NEED	
WORDS — HONEY COME BACK WHATEVER HAPPENED (BABY) TO YOU AND I		WORDS — HONEY COME BACK WHATEVER HAPPENED (BABY) TO YOU AND I	
STEREO **AL MARTINO** Capitol LP Album — CAN'T HELP FALLING IN LOVE STEREO	STEREO	**AL MARTINO** Capitol LP Album — CAN'T HELP FALLING IN LOVE	STEREO
SWEET CAROLINE — MY WAY YOU'RE ALL THE WOMAN THAT I NEED		SWEET CAROLINE — MY WAY YOU'RE ALL THE WOMAN THAT I NEED	

nostalgically about his good fortune as a singer and went on to lip-synch his new album's featured tune "Come Share the Wine," which, with luck, may go on to add to his vast repertoire of fine songs. Al had just returned from a tour in England and was soon heading back to tour one of his favorite venues, Germany, where he is so revered and returns there to perform annually.

Al Martino Speaks From Home

In 1994, Al Martino was interviewed at his beautiful French Country home in Beverly Hills by Lifestyles Magazine. Here are the questions asked of Al by writer Gwen Yount Carden.

How long are you living in this house?

Twenty Six years. My wife Judi and I bought it the year we were married.

How did you meet?

We met when I took a trip on American Airlines. She was a stewardess. She strapped me in and, before I knew it, we were married.

Do you have children?

One daughter, Alison, who's twenty-four. She lives in our guest house.

Is she following in her father's footsteps?

She wants to be a musician. She hopes to be a drummer in an all-girl rock band.

We notice there's a lot of white in the house.

I love white. When we bought the house it was very dark both inside and out. I made the whole house white. We have a white piano, white floors, white bar and carpets, and even our cat is white. I guess it's because I like things clean. If I can see that it's white, I know it's clean. I'm a very methodical person. I can't stand dirt anywhere.

It sounds like you really enjoy your home.

I'm very domesticated. I've done a lot of construction work here. It's a hobby. I have practically renovated the house

137

myself.

What are some of the things?

I put a sandstone patio in my yard and built a palatial fountain. I've poured concrete, laid brick, that's the kind of work I did before I was a singer.

What else do you do around the house?

I cook.

Wow, you sound handy to have around. How much cooking do you do?

All of it when I'm in town, which is just fine with Judi. In fact, I'm working on a meal right now. We're having Tommy LaSorda over for dinner tonight.

What do you cook?

Things like escarole with beans, homemade pasta with pork and veal meatballs, endive salad and pork butts. I cook mostly Italian dishes. I never use recipes, though, I always improvise.

Do you sing while you cook?

No, but I sing in the shower.

Do you miss cooking when you're on the road?

No, because my contracts always specify that my accommodations include cooking facilities. I cook for myself at least two or three times a week right in the hotel.

Do you work a lot?

I work pretty much all year. Right now I don't have any openings for the next three months. I'm about to leave for Germany and Australia.

Do you have any plans to retire?

I hate the word "retire." I never plan to retire. Why

should I? Quit working and do what? I plan to sing right to the end.

AUTHORS CHOICE -THE BEST LIST

We have selected a list of albums we think are the very best material offered by Al Martino. They are our own personal favorites. These albums reflect most of the important works he recorded.

The Exciting Voice of Al Martino

Painted, Tainted Rose

I Love You Because

Living a Lie

I Love You More and More Every Day

We Could

Somebody Else is Taking My Place

My Cherie

Spanish Eyes

I Think I'll Go Somewhere and Cry Myself to Sleep

This is Love

This Love For You

Daddy's Little Girl

Mary in the Morning

This is Al Martino

Love is Blue

Michael John Roselli

Jimmy Roselli

Ol' Brown Eyes is Back and Still Breaking Hearts

When he was 14 and sang "Little Pal," people would cry like a baby.

In 1996, Neapolitan crooner Jimmy Roselli turned seventy. Another great singing talent from Hoboken, New Jersey, Jimmy is certainly a premier singer of Italian favorites. Until then, Jimmy had recorded over thirty albums and the one which says it all is *Let Me Sing and Be Happy*.

However, one song alone would certify Jimmy Roselli's validity as a true Italian troubadour: "When Your Old Wedding Ring was New," a signature song, although the words are in English. Everyone loves that recording and no one sings it like Jimmy Roselli. I guess it is the equivalent to Don Cornell's "It Isn't Fair," Tony Bennett's "I Left My Heart in San Francisco," Jerry Vale's "Al Di La," Julie La Rosa's "Anywhere I Wander," or Frank Sinatra's "My Way." That recording clearly changed Jimmy's life. The long, hard hours of playing small clubs and receiving very little compensation were finally paying off for him. According to my friend Anthony Di Florio III in a 1966 article written in the Italian Tribune:

"When Jimmy Roselli gets out in front of the spotlight, he gives his all - every minute with every song."

And, Don Cornell once told me that, to him, Jimmy was the best Italian singer of them all. Wherever Jimmy appears he sells out - at Westbury Music Fair, Atlantic City, Florida, or Las Vegas - everywhere.

141

When Your Old Wedding Ring Was New

Bert Douglas, Charles McCarthy, Joseph Solieri

When your old wedding ring was new
And each dream that I dreamed came true
I remember with pride,
How we stood side by side
What a beautiful picture you made as my bride
Even though silver crowns your hair
I can still see the gold ringlets there
Love's old flame is the same
As the day I changed your name
When your old wedding ring was new.

Jimmy was born in Hoboken, New Jersey on December 26, 1925, two hours too late to have been born on Christmas Day. Sadly, he lost his mother the next day. Grandfather "Papa" Roselli raised him, along with his beloved (two) aunts, all instilling in him much love and an appreciation of music. Papa Roselli would take his grandson to hear local Italian opera. He renamed his grandson simply "Jimmy." Jimmy began singing in earnest in the church choir and later in the Gay Nineties Room at the local Meyers Hotel. Here, in Hoboken, Frank Sinatra lived at 415 Monroe Street and Jimmy at 514 Monroe Street, although they were ten years apart in age. At the age of thirteen, Jimmy was a first prize winner in a *Major Bowes Amateur Hour* contest, exactly where his rival Frank Sinatra received his first break. He sang the earlier Crosby favorite "Pocketful of Dreams" and won.

The Second World War summoned Jimmy to military duty. He served with the 266th Infantry. His need to sing, even then, was fulfilled on radio from Linz, Austria, while with the 42nd Rainbow Division Band, as well as with a swing band at the GIs' nightclub. Discharged in 1945, he took singing lessons and went on to perform throughout the East coast where he became a favorite, especially in New York City's *Little Italy*, thanks in part to unexpected help from the great, lovable and immensely popular singer and entertainer, Jimmy Durante, who encouraged Jimmy Roselli and even solicited the management of the famed Latin Quarter night club in Boston to increase his salary and extend his engagement. Success, time, chance, and opportunity was now at hand for the fledgling young singer.

Jimmy Roselli went on to play all the big clubs in and around New York, including a major appearance, later in 1964, at the famed Copacabana, with a response so fantastic that the management extended his four week engagement into a seven year record-breaking contract. Jimmy's first Carnegie Hall appearance on September 12, 1966 was completely sold out. "Mala Femmina," as arranged by Ralph Burns, (who also directed his Italian Album) is a recording that has endeared Jimmy to millions of Italian Americans. It was that recording that placed Jimmy firmly on the charts. His solid phrasing and song production won over future fans. Happy that he reached success with that recording, Jimmy was so excited that he would actually try to sell records from the trunk of his car to anyone he met. Ralph Burns also directed Jimmy's *Italian Album*.

According to Jimmy's biographer David Evanier, in order to be able to learn to correctly sing in a Neapolitan style:

"Jimmy used to frequent a store on Mulberry Street (in New York City) called the Italian Book Company. The couple who owned it were Neapolitans. Roselli asked for their help in the pronunciation and the phrasing of Neapolitan lyrics. They graciously gave him records from Italy with the melodies he was searching for. He learned the classics, what Jimmy calls the 'Stardust' of the Italian catalogue."

Jimmy spent much time listening to the recordings and tried to perfect his pronunciations. He wanted to become the best interpreter of Italian songs in the business. And he did!

This, of course, was the beginning of the 1960s when strong competition emerged from rock performers. This phenomenon stymied the progress of established singers who had to mark time and still try to retain their position in the down spiraling musical marketplace. Italian singers and their counterparts shifted their efforts to surfacing venues like Las Vegas where their fans flocked to see them perform in the various hotel lounges. Las Vegas appearances saved them from a sure demise. It was a place they could gather to perform and greet their faithful who traveled across the country to see them perform in person. Record companies exploited the new, rock and roll style entertainers and generally ignored established performers. The music didn't matter to them, they were accountants who simply looked at the bottom line. It became difficult for new, mainstream singers to get started. Established stars like Sinatra, Dean Martin, and Perry Como turned to television. Clearly, the kids who bought most of the records turned to their new heroes.

> *Jerry Vale: "Many years have passed since my so-to-speak 'heyday,' when I was a household word to my contemporaries. Now, at this time of my life, I am aware that my fans have been growing older along with me. Today's young adults may not know who Jerry Vale is, and why should they? They have their own musical heroes. There is no reason they should know who I am, although early twenties people sometimes show up at my concerts. For that I am grateful. I am also gratified for the legion of fans who have stuck with me throughout the years who are still there."*

In any case, Jimmy Roselli did pretty well in the 1960s with best selling albums and performing at premier places like Palumbo's in Philadelphia and annually at the Copacabana in New York.

When his contract with United Artists expired, Jimmy shrewdly negotiated a deal to take his valuable masters with him and created M & R Records, his own label, in Jersey City, New Jersey. He released his old albums and continued to record. Important engagements in England led to new recordings there with arranger/conductor Pete Moore. His album of *Saloon Songs* was the fruitful result. Jimmy has always excelled at performing these sentimental Neapolitan ballads which he first learned growing up at the knee of his loving grandfather.

Jimmy Roselli - *The Best of Neapolitan Songs.* His best Selling Italian album.

Song List:

Mala Femmina, Nun'a Penzo Proprio Cchiu, Piscatore 'E Pusilleco, Vint'Anne, Guaglione, Dimme Addo' Staje, Simmo 'E Napule, Paisa', Torna, Passione Ardente, Dooje Stelle So'Cadute, Statte Vicino Amme, Cienta Catene, Anema E Core, Ave Maria, Na Sera'e Maggio, Aria'e Pussilleco, Passione, Munasterio's Santa Chiara, 'Atazza'e Cafe, Pecche'si Femmina, Vierno, and Dicitencello Vuie.

Jimmy's *Italian Album* contains some of the best Italian songs: Tutta Pe'Mme, Innamorata, Scapricciatiello, Torna A Surriento, Aggio Perduto'o Suonno, Catena, Lusingame, 'Na Voce, 'Na Chitarra E'O Pogo'Eluna, Rusella 'E Maggio, 'O Paese D'O Sole, Che T'Aggia Di!

In 1998, David Evanier wrote the successful book *Making the Wiseguys Weep, The Jimmy Roselli Story.* It is a compelling book with no apologies and interesting biographical material. Within, Jimmy's son-in-law, Herb Bernstein, states, with respect to Jimmy's fame, that: "Of everyone in the U.S....maybe twenty-five million Italian people worship the ground he (Jimmy) walks on and the other two hundred million have never heard of him."

David, himself, fell in love with Jimmy's distinct sound: "I encountered him in person at the Westbury Music Fair in 1987; a simple, plain looking, unsophisicated man whose performance was one of the most moving experiences I had ever had since seeing Judy Garland at the Palace, or Sinatra or Ray Charles in concert. He has a powerful, authentic, commanding presence, a profound simplicity. The effect is thrilling when he sings with the huge orchestra."

And, David, who spoke to Jimmy regularly while writing his book, relates:

"When I came to know him better, Roselli, who has felt a rivalry with Sinatra his whole life, told me with a certain dispassion that he was puzzled that Sinatra continued to perform when most of his voice was gone. He said with certainty that the moment he (Jimmy) lost his voice, he would pack it in and retire."

"I'll fall down to give all that's in my body.
Because they came, they paid for that and they
deserve it. They should get the best that's in me."

Well, today, living in Florida with his wife Donna, Jimmy continues to travel up to the Connecticut casino's at Mohegan Sun and Foxwoods Resorts and performs for his faithful who make their short trip from New York and New Jersey. His voice still retains the strength and production it always enjoyed when at his peak. In late October, 2004, Jimmy Roselli returned to Long Island's Westbury Music Fair where he sang his great songs with a big orchestra, like he's always done. I hope you got to hear him once more.

Jimmy Durante with Roselli

Jimmy with his beloved aunts, Anne, Frieda, and Antonetta

Jimmy with his daughter, Anne Roselli Bernstein

with his wife Donna

Photos Courtesy David Evanier

147

☆AN EVENING WITH

BUDDY GRECO

The Green Room

AT THE CAFE ROYAL

Armando Greco

Buddy Greco

Benny Goodman's Protégé- Still Playing and Singing.

Another successful classical, musical product of Philadelphia is jazz piano playing-vocalist Buddy Greco, who began working at fifteen in his own trio in 1941. He named them *Three Shades of Rhythm*. Buddy's dad had freelanced as an opera performance critic all while managing his own popular record shop, as well as hosting his own radio show on WPEN, Philadelphia. Buddy loved to listen to the records of the Big Bands at his dad's shop, specifically the Benny Goodman swing band. Buddy studied classical piano at the famous Philadelphia Settlement House. While playing in a trio in 1948 at Philadelphia's Club 13, Buddy was scouted by Benny Goodman's band manager, leading to Buddy's playing in the band by the end of that year.

Playing piano, arranging, and singing in that great Goodman organization, was a dream come true for the young musician. His ultra-hip interpretations of classy songs fit in nicely with the ever-expanding Goodman band.

During the following few years, Buddy recorded dozens of sides with Benny and would sometimes lead the band while on overseas engagements.

When Benny Goodman first hired Buddy in 1948, Buddy was riding a rocket with his own trio's recording of Carmen Lombardo's "Ooh! Look-a -There, Ain't She Pretty?" with Buddy on the vocal.

"I received only thirty-two dollars for that recording," he said. However, Buddy didn't feel so bad after learning the Andrews Sisters received only fifty-dollars for their blockbuster recording of "Bie Mir Bist du Shoen" and had to split it three ways, and that vocalist Fran Warren received but fifty dollars for her great hit "Sunday Kind of Love" recorded with Claude Thornhill's orchestra.

"After the record "O-o-h Looka There.." was released, a lot

of leaders wanted me to join their band, but I was never interested. But when Benny called, I responded. I had always admired him and I wanted to learn my profession the best way possible. So, I gave up a lot of bucks to go with Benny. For some obscure reason Benny took a liking to me."

Benny knew that Buddy had come from poor circumstances in South Philadelphia:

"But, he also knew I had won a scholarship to Curtis Institute when I was fourteen and I think that impressed him.

The first thing Benny had Buddy play at his audition for the band was a serious classical piece:

"He just threw it in front of me like nothing. And I played it, and that afternoon he took me to meet the great Igor Stravinsky. And, Benny knew I had perfect pitch."

When Buddy became comfortable with the band, he would invoke some mischievous musical nonsense now and then: "As a tease, sometimes I would change the key on the introduction to certain songs, and he wouldn't be able to catch it right away, so he'd come in on the original key, then look over his glasses and give me the famous Benny Goodman 'ray.' He must have fired me ten times during the year and a half I was with him, then promptly hired me back with a raise each time."

Buddy's overall relationship with the unusual personality of Goodman combined with his own mercurial self was generally good. "Sometimes he would invite me to stay with his wife and kids at their apartment in New York. He would also send money to my parents, which wasn't typical of him. Who would do such a thing? To me Benny was always kind and generous and I loved him for that."

During his time with Goodman, Buddy Greco introduced specially arranged bebop and modern jazz material into the band's book. During an engagement at the Hollywood Palladium, Buddy had to take over directing the orchestra when Benny suddenly took ill with a bad back and had to leave the podium, signaling Buddy to take the stand and lead the band.

Buddy traveled to London with Benny to perform with a London based orchestra because the British Musicians Union would not permit the entire band to come over to play. The band, fronted by Goodman, with Buddy as piano player, received rave reviews, even though pick-up musicians were rounded up to form a musically valid jazz band. These musicians knew the Goodman book and just how to play it.

Jerry Vale and Buddy Greco (J. Vale Collection)

A year later, Benny Goodman disbanded, complaining that "The music was different for him and he would rather play the early stuff." Buddy said,

"Overall and after working it a bit, Benny thought the bop material was wrong for the future of his kind of music, and decided he was through with it."

Benny Goodman once told me the happiest times with his band was back in the *Bluebird* recording days.

"I think those days were my best musically and the music was good." He was appearing at a *Salute to Benny Goodman Day* show on radio station WLIM on Long Island in 1982. "I loved the early days of swing when I was developing my style and making records that people still love and play."

In the early fifties, Buddy began writing tunes for other singers, like Rosemary Clooney, and performing on his own radio show. When I was with NBC Guest Relations in the early fifties, I remember Buddy working on the Jerry Lester late night forerunner of the *Tonight Show*, called *Broadway Open House,* with vocalist David Street and musical director Milton De Lugg. 1967 found Buddy's show as the summer replacement for Jackie Gleason's TV show. Buddy shared the show, co-starring with brilliant drummer Buddy Rich. It was named the "Away We Go!" series and featured many fine musicians and comedians.

To many, Buddy Greco is acknowledged as a Frank Sinatra style vocalist, performing all the classic tunes of the great composers in the 'bel canto' style, adding his own endings and vocal charm to performances.

The 1970s found Buddy living in Europe for a while, performing prolifically in appearances throughout Europe and down under the Equator in Australia.

This *singer's singer* has made 65 albums with so many diverse performers and in many genre's stretching from bop through country, including big band and ballads too. He has recorded 100 singles. He has played piano with the great London Symphony Orchestra and recorded with all the great, all-star musicians. The London recordings are his favorite, as he played, arranged and directed the orchestra. In 1955, Buddy recorded with vocalist compatriots Alan Dale and Johnny Desmond on Coral, and was featured on television programs starring singer Andy Williams, comedian-dancer Donald O'Connor and pianist, composer, and host Steve Allen.

Buddy's last notable work was performing at revered Carnegie Hall for a tribute to his friend, pianist and vocalist, the wonderful Nat "King" Cole.

AUTHORS CHOICE

Buddy's Best

At Long Last Love
Call Me Irresponsible
It Had Better Be Tonight (meglio sta sera)
Teach me Tonight
Something's Gotta Give
Around the World in Eighty Days
The Lady is a Tramp
It Isn't Fair
Don't Worry About Me
The Land of Oo-Bla-Dee
Brother Bill

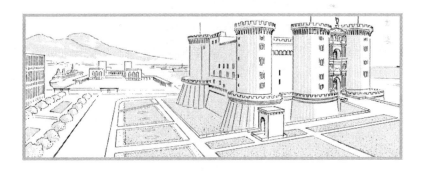

CLEMENTINE

by WOODY HARRIS

THE ORIGINAL VERSION

AS RECORDED ON LONDON H L 9086

BY BOBBY DARIN

 SOUTHERN MUSIC PUBLISHING Co. Ltd.,
8 Denmark Street, London, W.C.2

2/-

154

Walden Robert Cassotto

Bobby Darin- Mighty Mighty Man - Gone too Soon

Whenever I hear the *Three Penny Opera* classic "Mack the Knife" I think, of course, of Bobby Darin and the great rendition that established him for all time. (Not that's there is anything wrong with Louis Armstrong's version). The same goes for the tunes "Clementine" and "Beyond the Sea." It also seems that all Darin's recordings were performed upbeat, utilizing many types of rhythms. Maybe Bobby knew his life would be cut short and so he tried to get as much of music and life in as possible. In the seventeen years he recorded, he sure packed in every genre of product available to him in the business.

Born in 1936 and sadly gone in 1973, Bobby Darin was a confident force in music like very few before or after him. Influenced mostly by Frank Sinatra, he began as a rock and roller, drummer and piano player, and worked up into the great music standards by way of pop country, gospel, swing, and jazz. Regardless of style, Bobby Darin tried everything - a one of a kind performer.

Bobby performed at the Copacabana, recorded an album with the great composer/lyricist Johnny Mercer, backed by legendary Billy May, and performed mightily on television and in films.

Born on May 14,1936, Bobby was a prime product of the Bronx, New York, but, unfortunately contracted dreaded rheumatic fever as a little kid, an illness that damaged his heart and was the eventual cause of his passing in December, 1973.

Bobby was obsessed with making an early name for himself in show business. After graduating high school and attending a year of college, he became a demo writer and singer at the famous Brill Building in New York, the heart and soul of Tin Pan Alley, where songwriters, song pluggers, arrangers and publishers gathered to offer their wares in written and recorded music to all the world. Bobby Darin's first hits, both that he wrote himself, were with

Atco Records with the release of "Splish Splash" (written with Jean Murray in 1958) and "Dream Lover" in 1959. This success followed up with an album entitled *That's All*, a sturdy compilation of standards performed in the unmistakable Darin style and featured what was to become his biggest hit, "Mack the Knife." Well, he won two Grammy's as both *Record of the Year* and was cited as *Best New Artist*, and he never looked back. He was like the little engine that would, could - and did.

Bobby was twenty-three when he was invited to important career boosting engagements in musically teeming Las Vegas and at the famed Copacabana in New York, where all the great performers of his day were sooner or later engaged. Besides singing in his act, Bobby also performed remarkable impressions and played piano. He successfully welded together swing with rhythm and blues, with rock in-between.

Bobby Darin

A prolific actor, composer, and vocalist, Bobby Darin did it all, and in record time. He appeared in no less than thirteen films, had his own television variety program (1972 and '73), composed a startling number of songs, some for motion pictures and others for popular recordings. He led Las Vegas star Wayne Newton to success when he suggested to him the song "Danke Schoen". You see - Bobby, always grateful, gave something back.

First married to actress Sandra Dee, his co-star in *Come September*, with whom he had a son, Dodd Darin, and then a second marraige to Andrea Yaeger. Bobby Darin passed in

December 1973 when he was only thirty-seven years old. But, what a career he created in such a short time. In 1990, he was posthumously inducted into the *Rock and Roll Hall of Fame* and into the *Songwriters Hall of Fame* in 1999, and in that same year his prolific and exciting life and career were documented on Public Television.

Today, Darin still thrives in the minds and lives of many including his devoted son Dodd, who, like Kathryn Crosby, pursues to establish an everlasting legacy for her husband, Bing Crosby, works at securing a place in music history for his dad with help from Darin's close friend, and publicist, Harriet Wasser. The award winning actor Kevin Spacey, a great Darin fan, motivated by a solemn promise to his mother in her final days, finished making a film in Germany of Bobby Darin's life to be entitled *Beyond the Sea*. The film will be released just about the time this book goes to press, November 2004.

Author's Choice - Some of Bobby Darin's Greatest Hits

The Top Ten

1. Mack the Knife
2. Beyond the Sea
3. Clementine
4. Artificial Flowers
5. Won't You Come Home Bill Bailey
6. If I Were a Carpenter
7. Dream Lover
8. Love Come Back to Me
9. A Nightingale Sang in Berkeley Square
10. Mame

Bobby's best albums are *The Very Best of Bobby Darin* with thirty of his best recordings, and *Two of a Kind* with thirteen selections and the combination of Johnny Mercer, one of our best song writers and the direction of Billy May and his orchestra.

158

Frank Wayne Sinatra

Frank Sinatra, Jr. - *His Sisters call Him Frankie.*

It's hard to write about the son of the great Frank Sinatra. Frank Jr. has been a skilled vocalist, piano player and bandleader in his own right for years, but most of his life always under the giant shadow of his dad where it had to be difficult to exist comfortably as a singer.

Nevertheless, Frankie continued on his way, despite conflicts within himself. He was born in 1944 in Jersey City, New Jersey, and learned violin and piano at an early age and even attended boarding school while his father established his legendary career. Frankie always took ordinary jobs until April 28, 1962 when he performed publicly on the piano for the first time. The following year he performed at Disneyland in California with the house band. The musicians liked him and asked him to come back for a Dorsey Band tribute a few days later where he sang his dad's old standards "I'll Never Smile Again," "Yes, Indeed," and "There Are Such Things." The crowd loved it.

His debut album, *Young Love for Sale*, on his dad's Reprise label was a collection of very nice ballads, surprisingly first-rate. "It was the best I had to offer," Frankie said at the time, considering he was always compared to his dad's fine works. Frankie toured incessantly through the sixties and performed on television and had his own CBS hour long special in 1969. His dad and sister, Nancy, joined in the show, along with old friend Jack Benny, and Sammy Davis, Jr. Great support, I'd say.

Frankie continued to record and perform throughout the 1970s and into the 1980s. In 1982, he worked on a Billy May tribute album with bandleader Pat Longo. Billy May, trumpeter, arranger, bandleader, had backed Frank Sr. on a number of albums. Frankie continued performing regularly with his live act, accompanied by stellar musicians concentrating on big band favorites, trying always to set aside his dad's famed material, even though he received many requests otherwise.

In 1988, Frankie worked closely with his dad, accompanying him as musical director during his final years of performing. He sang in the Duet's album with his dad on the song "My Kind of Town."

1996 was the year Frankie released his full-blown album called *As I Remember It* on CD. It was his first recording in some 20 years. Within, in addition to 32 song tracks, he personally recounts the Frank Sinatra story very succinctly and passionately, as only a son who has been there is able to remember and present it when there is love and respect from an appreciative son to a father. Because he had absorbed the almost identical shades of his father's timing, expressions, and stage presence, he could authentically create this album.

Frankie Sinatra is really his own man. Sure, he had help ordinary people could not expect to receive. But, he has worked hard for his success and has tried not to live in his father's shadow, or cash in on this father's career, however difficult that must be. He is currently performing and touring, and has even appeared on the television series, *The Sopranos*. I imagine, with health, Frankie will continue to sing with a quality orchestra and sing quality music for many years.

Frankie always fills the house wherever his engagements take him, whether in New York, Atlantic City, or Las Vegas, or anywhere else, you can expect to hear his lifelong quest to perform quality music. As this book goes to print, the Frankie Sinatra scheduled itinerary continues on.

In the final analysis, Frankie is a chip, though a more gentle chip, off the old block. The old block being his dad - the one and only Frank Sinatra.

This fine singer and musician can now carry on the great Sinatra musical tradition.

A Salute To The Singer and Their Songs

READERS AND CRITICS POLL OF FAVORITE

SONGS RECORDED BY ITALIAN

CROONERS OVER THE YEARS

Submitted by Author Richard Grudens:

1. Al Di La - Jerry Vale
2. Eh! Compari - Julius La Rosa
3. Volare - Dean Martin
4. When Your Old Wedding Ring was New - Jimmy Roselli
5. It Isn't Fair - Don Cornell
6. Anema E Core - Perry Como
7. Because of You - Tony Bennett
8. I Believe - Frankie Laine
9. Angelina - Louis Prima
10. In the Wee Small Hours of the Morning - Frank Sinatra

Submitted by noted author and critic, Anthony DeFlorio III:

1. O Sole Mio-Jerry Vale
2. Pepino, the Italian Mouse-Lou Monte
3. Non Ti Scordar Di Me-Carlo Buti
4. Oh, Marie (Slow version)-Louis Prima and chorus
5. Darktown Strutters Ball-Lou Monte
6. Mala Femmena-Jimmy Roselli
7. Anema E Core-Perry Como
8. Oh Marie (fast version)-Louis Prima
9. Mama-Connie Francis
10. Volare-Domenico Mondugno

Submitted by Gregory Mario Jacovini, Publisher The Italian Newspaper (Artists not noted):

1.   Simmo 'E Napule, Paisa
2.   Mala Femmena
3.   L'Italiano
4.   Bella Ciao
5.   Volare
6.   Core 'Ngrato
7.   'O Surdato 'Nnammurato
8.   La Luna Mezzo Mare
9.   Tu Vuo' Fa' L'Americano
10.   Dicitencello Vuje

Submitted by Jimmy Scalia of The Official Bobby Darin Archivist (Artists not noted):

1.   Perdere L'Ampre
2.   Caruso
3.   Return to Me
4.   Mama
5.   Anema E Core
6.   Al Di La
7.   Mala Femmena
8.   Sorrento
9.   An Evening in Rome
10.   Lazy Mary

Submitted by Record Producer and band vocalist of <u>Blue Dahlia</u>, Athan Maroulis:

1.   In the Wee Small Hours of the Morning-Frank Sinatra
2.   Prisoner of Love - Russ Columbo
3.   That's My Desire - Frankie Laine
4.   Temptation - Perry Como
5.   I've Grown Accustomed to Your Face - Tony Bennett
6.   Arrivederci Roma - Jerry Vale
7.   I Have But One Heart - Vic Damone
8.   Buona Sera - Louis Prima
9.   Beyond the Sea - Bobby Darin
10.   Volare - Dean Martin

Submitted by Composer/Lyricist Ervin Drake:

1.   I Believe - Frankie Laine
2.   It Was a Very Good Year - Frank Sinatra
3.   Castle Rock - Frank Sinatra
4.   Al Di La - Jerry Vale
5.   Father of Girls - Perry Como
6.   Sonata - Perry Como
7.   I Have But One Heart - Vic Damone
8.   You're Breaking My Heart -
9.   Here in My Heart - Al Martino
10. That's Amore - Dean Martin

Notice: Ervin Drake wrote the first six songs above. " See how partial I am to my own songs?" he wrote when submitting his list.

Submitted by Malcolm Macfarlane
Editor Bing Crosby International Magazine, London, England:

1.   Return to Me - Dean Martin
2.   Come Back to Sorrento - Dean Martin
3.   There's No Tomorrow (O Sole Mio) - Dean Martin
4.   Santa Lucia - Perry Como
5.   Anema e Core - Perry Como
6.   That's Amore - Dean Martin
7.   Ciao Ciao Bambina - Jerry Vale
8.   Arriverderci Roma - Perry Como
9.   Oh! Marie - Perry Como
10. Volare - Dean Martin

Submitted by Max Wirz, famed Swiss Eviva radio Host:

1.   Granada - Frankie Laine
2.   I Believe - Frankie Laine
3.   Because of You - Tony Bennett
4.   Far Away Places - Perry Como
5.   Come Back to Sorrento - Don Cornell
6.   Angela Mia - Vic Damone
7.   That's Amore - Dean Martin
8.   Spanish Eyes - Al Martino
9.   Buena Sera - Louis Prima
10.   Arrivederci Roma - Jerry Vale

Submitted by Ben Grisafi, Bandleader and Musical Director of the Big Band Hall of Fame and Museum, Palm Beach, Florida:

1.   Inammorata - Jerry Vale
2.   New York, New York - Frank Sinatra
3.   On the Street Where You Live - Vic Damone
4.   I'm in the Mood for Love - Al Martino
5.   Hey, Compari - Julius La Rosa
6.   Mala Femmena - Jimmy Roselli
7.   Till the End of Time - Perry Como
8.   Al Di La - Jerry Vale
9.   When Your Old Wedding Ring was New - Jimmy Roselli
10. I Believe - Frankie Laine

Submitted by Singer/Pianist John Primerano:

1.   Al Di La - Jerry Vale
2.   Mala Femmena - Jerry Vale
3.   Just Say I Love Her - Jerry Vale
4.   I Have But One Heart - Vic Damone
5.   You're Breaking My Heart - Vic Damone
6.   Mama - Jerry Vale
7.   Volare - Dean Martin
8.   Here in My Heart - Al Martino
9.   Mala Femmena - Jimmy Roselli
10. From the Vine Came the Grape - The Gaylords

Submitted by Al Monroe, New Jersey WNTI Radio Personality & V.P.; New York Chapter Society of Singers:

1.   That's Amore - Dean Martin
2.   Volare - Dean Martin
3.   Non Dimenticar - Vic Damone
4.   Innamorata - Dean Martin
5.   Arrivederci Roma - Jerry Vale
6.   Al Di La - Jerry Vale
7.   Come Back to Sorrento - Frank Sinatra
8.   Anema E Core - Don Cornell
9.   Mala Femmena - Don Cornell
10. Funiculi Funicula - Sergio Franchi

Submitted by Filippo Voltaggio - Italian Style Vocalist:

1.   Round and Round - Perry Como
2.   Innamorata - Dean Martin

3.   Come Fly with Me - Frank Sinatra
4.   I Left My Heart in San Francisco - Tony Bennett
5.   Buona Sera - Louis Prima
6.   Spanish Eyes - Al Martino
7.   Just Say I Love Her (Dicitencello Vuie)
8.   Italian Christmas Donkey - Louis Monte
9.   Some Enchanted Evening - Ezioi Pinza
10. Arriverderci - Mario Lanza

Submitted by Vocalist Wynne Miller (Vocalist and Niece of Glenn MIller):

1.   Angela Mia - Vic Damone
2.   It's Impossible - Perry Como
3.   All The Way - Frank Sinatra
4.   In the Cool, Cool, Cool of the Evening - Dean Martin
5.   I Wanna Be Around - Bobby Darin
6.   All Right, Louie, Drop the Gun - Louis Prima
7.   We'll Be Together Again - Frankie Laine
8.   Baby Face - Jimmy Roselli
9.   Mala Femmina - Jerry Vale
10. Band of Gold - Don Cornell

Submitted by Big Band Vocalist Connie Haines

1.   Catch a Falling Star - Perry Como
2.   Snootie Little Cutie - Frank Sinatra (with Connie Haines)
3.   Two Purple Shadows - Jerry Vale
4.   Pretend You Don't See Her - Jerry Vale
5.   Heart of my Heart - Don Cornell
6.   Mack the Knife - Bobby Darin
7.   Be My Love - Mario Lanza
8.   Volare - Dean Martin
9.   Spanish Eyes - Al Martino
10. Let's Get Away from it All - Frank Sinatra (with Connie Haines)

Submitted by Ann Jillian - Broadway star, television and film actress, and a very good singer in her own right, and her husband Andy Murcia. Ann honors Connie Francis in her own act with a medley of Connie's songs. Check her web at www.AnnJillian.com. This list represents their favorite performers:

1. Jimmy Roselli - When Your Old Wedding Ring was New, and everything he does.
2. Perry Como - Ave Maria. Mr. Smooth, we adored his singing. Ann did his Easter Special and loved him dearly.
3. Jerry Vale - AL DI LA . We adore his singing and the man himself - a first class gent.
4. Mario Lanza - Not his operatic material, but his love songs like Be My Love.
5. Dean Martin - Everybody Loves Somebody. Always tops.
6. Al Martino - Mary in the Morning. Every Italian restaurant in Chicago had him on the jukebox. We like his style.
7. Vic Damone - An Affair to Remember. A very nice guy and a steady singer.
8. Tony Bennett - Because of You. Not in Italian, but in English he's the best.
9. Frank Sinatra - New York, New York, of course!
10. Frankie Laine - That's My Desire. A great guy and last saw him at his home in San Diego a few years ago when he was still singing.

Submitted by Megan West - Big Band Leader in the Glenn Miller Style

1. Mala Femmena - Mimmy Roselli
2. Please No Squeeza the Banana - Louie Prima
3. Lazy Mary - Lou Monte
4. Girl Talk - Buddy Greco
5. Spanish Eyes - Al Martino
6. More - Steve Rossi
7. O Solo Mio - Tony Bennett
8. Eh! Cumpari - Julius LaRosa
9 Because You're Mine - Mario Lanza
10. Beyond the Sea - Bobby Darin

Italian Proverbs

BY FLORENCE SCALFANI

IL Maestro Cambia La Musica La Stessa.
The conductor may changes but the music remains the same.

Canta E Passa.
Sing and it will pass.

Vivo per la Musica.
I Live for the Music.

NEAPOLITAN PROVERBS

A cavallo rialato nun se guarda 'mmocca.
Every gift, even if modest, always has an intrinsic value and so it has always to be well accepted and appreciated.

'A cicala canta, canta e po' schiatta.
The superficial people enjoy themselves continually and then they have a bad end.

Addo' vaje truove guaje.
Unfortunately the world is afflicted with thousands of troubles and everyone has his trouble.

A dicere so' tutte capace; 'o defficile e a ffa.
Between saying and making there is the sea in the middle.

CALABRESE PROVEREBS

L'unita fa la forza.
Unity makes strength.

Stipate u pane, no de fatica.
Put your bread aside (to save) never your chores.

A tuttu ci'e riparu..abasta cu'n sonna la campana..che a la morte sullu un ci'e riparu!
For all problems, save the tolling of the bell, there are solutions. Death alone is without solutions.

U gutaru continuu, bucca la petra.
A constant water drip will pierce a stone.

A superbia arriva a cavallo e pue ritorna a pieri.
Arrogance arrives on horseback but returns on foot.

SICILIAN PROVERBS

Cu mancia fa muddichi.
A person eating must make crumbs.
Idiom: You have to break a few eggs to make an omelette.

Cu gaddu e senza gaddu, diu fa journa.
God will make the sun rise with or without the rooster.
Idiom: Give credit where credit is due.

Nun si po' aviri la carni senz' ossu.
You can't have the meat without the bone.
Idiom: Take the good with the bad.

Camina chi pantofuli finu a quannu non hai i scarpi.
Walk with your slippers until you find your shoes.
Idiom: Make due with what you got (make the best of a bad situation).

Frank Sinatra and Bing Crosby in "High Society"

"*You must be one of the newer fellers!*"

You may remember Bing Crosby and Frank Sinatra in that singing duet scene in a mansion, in the house bar, during the film *High Society,* when Bing declared to Frank at one point, "You must be one of the newer fellers!"

We have noticed there is quite a legion of new Italian Crooners out there looking for work. We start with Tony "Tony B" Babino.

Anthony Babino

TONY BABINO

Tony "B" — A Singing Storm Who Keeps the Music Going Strong.

Tony B. might just be the classic trailblazing, high-energy vocalist of the new Millennium. His qualifications match those of all the up-and-coming singers of past generations, in a time identified as before and during the Big Band Era, and beyond. Those were the days when the great Al Jolson and the prolific crooner Bing Crosby had established the era of the vocalists and cleared the way for followers Frank Sinatra, Perry Como, Jerry Vale, Don Cornell, Eddie Fisher, Johnny Mathis, Vic Damone, Al Martino, Tony Bennett, and a dozen worthy others, all who tossed their vocal skills into the ring to compete for the gold in the shape of a shellac recording. Tony B. and his counterparts are a distinct extension of those fledgling careers. Are those days about to resurface? Is the world ready for good music again? It will, if Tony B. has his way. He's trying to bring it all back.

In his quest for excellence in performing Tony B. has carefully surrounded himself with qualified people in his arena, from personal manager Robert Rosenblatt, who believes in his client unconditionally and has provided unwavering support in matters both legal and career; to arranger and premier piano accompanist Richie Iacona, whose arrangements, as Tony B. states: "...breathe new life into classic standards, but give my own original compositions the edge they need to stand on their own within the genre.'"

The friendship of the incomparable Connie Haines, who sang shoulder-to-shoulder with Frank Sinatra in the bands of Harry James and Tommy Dorsey for three years as they grew together in music performing, has bolstered Tony B.'s career to an even higher plateau. He sang with Connie in Florida before over ten thousand fans:

"From the moment I met Connie, she took me under

173

her wing and made me feel like family. She is a wonderful and beautiful person, and her talent is second to none. That lady can swing, baby! When we'd perform in Atlantic City night after night she'd invite me up on stage, not only to perform, but to share the spotlight. There aren't too many performers in this business who would extend an opportunity like that to someone new. May God bless and keep her, always."

Tony B. began singing at a very young age after first being impressed by Bobby Darin's knockout recording of "Mack the Knife." Previously, he worshipped heroes Al Jolson, Frank Sinatra, Tony Bennett and Paul McCartney. Tony B.'s impressions of Al Jolson are simply unbelievable and matched to perfection. Tony B.'s counterparts today are versed in the sounds of Michael Buble', Peter Cincotti, Harry Connick,

Tony and Connie Haines at the Three Village Inn, Stonybrook, New York, 2002 - (B. Grisafi Photo)

Jr., John Primerano, and Filippo Voltaggio. Tony's power and production are overpowering and contain a punch that knocks you out. He is a Sinatra, a Darin, a Bennett, and a Jolson, if you will, all in one.

Last February, I invited Tony B. to an interview at my local haunt, the Three Village Inn in Stonybrook, New York. Tony and I first met there when I hosted a book signing and luncheon for big band vocalist Connie Haines a year earlier. I had written Connie's biography "Snootie Little Cutie" the year before. After lunch, Tony and Connie spontaneously launched a performance from their *Stars and Stripes Revue* show. Connie was presented with a Lifetime Achievement Award from the prestigeous Five Towns College Music School on Long Island.

After lunch and some introspective interview conversation, Tony provided my wife, Madeline, with an impromptu *a capella* version of Jolson singing "When the Red, Red, Robin Comes Bob Bob Bobbin' Along." Well, the power and phrasing, as well as the distinctly accurate performance was amazing. As we applauded, we became aware of a sizable gathering who had worked their way into our dining area when they heard his powerful interpretation of the great Jolson resonate throughout this great old inn without the use of a microphone.

Tony at the "Italia Mia" Luncheon, 2004 (M. Grudens Photo)

"When Tony Babino started to croon as Al Jolson, the packed house stopped breathing. You could have heard a pin drop...and when he dropped to his knees, all you could hear was a fabulous rendition of 'Sonny Boy.'"

The Trumball Times, Conn.

"Saturday evening, patrons of the Variety Art Center in L.A. were treated to a scintillating performance of Jolson standards by Tony Babino."

Daily Variety, Los Angles, Cal.

"I became interested in Al Jolson when I was just a kid. I was watching the Million Dollar Movie on our local Channel 9. They used to run the movie for an entire week, once during the day and once at night. One day, *The Jolson Story* came on, and from that moment, even though I was just a kid, I wanted to locate all the Jolson music that I could to listen to. I thought he was phenomenal. I think I watched every show that week. I was transfixed on Jolson and his music for life."

The phenomenon of the Beatles eclipsed his fixation on Jolson for a while. Some years later, at a relatives home, Tony discovered a Jolson album and played it and began imitating him until he had memorized every song.

"I bought some more Jolson material and began memorizing just about every song he ever recorded. I became obsessed with Jolson. I could even whistle like he did. I was in love with his songs and the way he sang them. After a while, people began to say that

Joan and Sam Arlen in their Commack, NY house (R. Grudens Photo)

I sounded like Jolson. That's how it all started. Today, I continue to sing Jolson at almost every performance." Tony produced a demo Jolson CD with four songs and original orchestrations. You cannot distinquish Tony B. from Al Jolson. Believe me!

Up to now, Tony B. has performed at

just about every important venue in Atlantic City. And his mounting credits to date span personal numerous performances, recordings, and total involvement in his trade. His recording of the Harold Arlen evergreen "Come Rain or Come Shine" was selected by Arlen's son, Sam and his wife, Joan, to be included on a Harold Arlen Songbook album, sharing tracks with Tony Bennett, Faith Hill, Eric Clapton, Jane Monheit and Natalie Cole. He is featured on the number one track.

> ### *"Tony B. is as exciting as Bobby Darin was when he first burst upon the scene."*
>
> *Joey Reynolds, host of WOR Radio Hall of Fame show.*

> *"After knocking them dead in the hit holiday show, "Ring-A-Ding Christmas" at the Sands Casino Hotel in Atlantic City, Tony B (Tony Babino) returned for one night only to stage a musical and comedy extravaganza on the same stage. The centerpiece of the evening was Tony's tribute to composer Harold Arlen, performing a medley arranged by Richie Iacona, who conducted the orchestra."*

Staten Island
Advance, April 25, 2004

Tony with Luisa Potenza (M. Grudens Photo)

In April, 2004, Tony appeared at a show for WALK radio's *Italia Mia* luncheon with hostess, Luisa Potenza. Luisa had interviewed Tony for her show and invited him, my wife Madeline and I to be guests. At the luncheon event I talked about the progress of this very book and fielded questions brought by the over 150 guests about their favorite Italian crooner with the emphasis on Jerry Vale, who seemed to be their favorite. I then introduced Tony B. to this small, but enthusiastic all-Italian audience and they simply went wild over his performance of Italian and other standards, including two Jolson favorites. They afforded him a standing ovation.

Swingin' Around is Tony B's 1999 CD with Richie Iacona playing a real quality piano and conducting the orchestra. Tony seems very much at home with Richie's piano nearby, especially on "Watch What Happens," "Till There was You," and "Almost Like Being in Love," all three the best of Tony B. It's an album worthy of comparing it to Sinatra sometimes and Darin other times. Both are ingrained in Tony's psyche. That's for sure.

Tony B. credits his wife Elaine for the full time expansion of his career as it stands.

"Elaine encouraged me to go full time after I experienced a negative, life threatening event in my life. She is the reason I have decided to expand my career and try to make it in this business. So far, so good. And I keep working at it day by day, week by week. Elaine is one hundred percent behind me. And for that I am grateful."

Tony and Elaine's two boys are already steeped in music. Anthony, 16, has been playing guitar since he was 9 years old, and Steven regularly appears in stage shows whenever he can, recently performing in a company of Frank Loesser's *Guys and Dolls* .

With much hard work still ahead, Tony B. knows he can do it. He's setting a standard for his kids as Sinatra set the standard for him. The music goes on. The Babino family does their share.

Swingin Around with Tony B

Arranged and conducted by Richie Iacona

I've Got the World on a String
Swingin Around
I've Gotta Get Back to New York
I Wish I Could Sing Like Sinatra
Til There was You
Watch What Happens
Sentimental Heartstrings
Back in Your Own Backyard
You Are Too Beautiful
Almost Like Being in Love
In the Wee Small Hours
And I Love Her
All of Me
Fifty Years

HAROLD ARLEN NOW!
Modern Recordings of Timeless Classics

This compact disc demonstrates 10 Harold Arlen compositions that are available for use in advertising, films, TV, radio, audio/visual and all media. Please see inlay card for details.

Visit the Official Harold Arlen Website at www.haroldarlen.com

FOR PROMOTIONAL USE ONLY

S.A. Music Co.
97 Croft Lane
Smithtown, NY 11787
Tel. (631) 360-2360.

1. I've Got The World On A String: TONY B.
2. Stormy Weather: ROYAL CROWN REVUE
3. Come Rain or Come Shine: ERIC CLAPTON AND B.B. KING
4. Ac-cent-tchu-ate the Positive: DR. JOHN
5. Blues in the Night: TONY BENNETT
6. I Gotta Right To Sing the Blues: FRANCINE REED
7. The Man That Got Away: FRANCINE REED
8. Hit the Road To Dreamland: JANE MONHEIT
9. It's Only A Paper Moon: NATALIE COLE
10. Over The Rainbow: FAITH HILL

Tony B. has Got the World on a String - on this Harold Arlen CD

180

John Primerano

Maybe Someday is today.
His Ancestors are from Calabria, Italy.

John Primerano is a one-of-a-kind Italian troubadour. He is in his 40's and plays and sings the entire book of the Golden Age of Music, including the works of Cole Porter, Richard Rodgers, Sammy Cahn, George and Ira Gershwin, Irving Berlin, Harold Arlen, Harry Warren, and dozens of other composers. John has even written a few tunes of his own, namely "Saloon Song," and "Maybe Someday." And, he has put them both on a single CD. They are both promising songs fit for a Sinatra, Bennett, or Roselli.

John is a soft spoken keyboard wizard who has virtually memorized practically every known song and *never* plays with the aid of sheet music that most piano players need in front of them when performing. John makes a living playing and singing in clubs mostly around the greater Philadelphia area. And, he is Italian, and his voice evokes the sounds of Roselli, Dick Haymes and sometimes Sinatra, himself.

My wife Madeline and I sat down at lunch with John Primerano at Stonybrook's Three Village Inn one afternoon in July, 2004. He came up to meet us from his home in Philadelphia for this interview and recounted snippets of his career which began when he was just a kid.

A few weeks later John joined us once again for an appearance at a luncheon sponsored by radio station WALK and hosted by *Italia Mia* personality, gracious and

Luisa Potenza and John Primerano at the Bavarian Inn, Long Island
(M. Grudens Photo)

popular Louisa Potenza, whose radio show airs on Sunday's from eleven to one.

181

MAYBE SOMEDAY

Music and Lyrics by John Primerano

Maybe someday you'll need me
Maybe someday you'll care
Maybe someday you'll want me to be there
There might come a time you'll miss me
When you think that your time's runnin' out
Maybe that's when you'll see what I'm all about

And maybe some night alone in your bed I'll creep into your mind
And maybe my voice will sound in your head
Giving life to mem'ries you thought you left behind
Maybe someday you'll find me
When you found what you're not lookin' for
Maybe that's when you'll knock upon my door and Maybe my heart won't live here anymore.

182

John played his heart out to an appreciative audience, especially when he played and sang a popular Italian medley that began with "Oh, Marie" and concluded with Ervin Drake's "Al Di La." I've never known any artist who could play and sing so effectively, except perhaps Nat "King" Cole, Bobby Short, or lately, Michael Feinstein, currently on the New York scene. I remember Nat's wife, Maria Cole, telling me how difficult playing and singing simultaneously was for her husband who perfected the art sitting askew on a piano bench turned away from the keyboard and never glancing back while playing those difficult jazz accompaniments. John adds further excitement to his piano with rippling arpeggios and amazing keyboard magic, never looking down as his melodies poured forth great music and those fingers serpentined back and forth over those black and white ivories.

John Primerano (M. Grudens Photo)

Born and raised in Philadelphia, John began piano lessons when he was eight and worked professionally as a piano accompanist for U.S.O. groups when he was just fifteen. He studied music, earning a degree in composition at Temple University's School of Music. Playing for a variety of singers over the years has forced John to become proficient in transposing songs to convenient or alternate keys on the spot.

"Sometimes a singer would have the sheet, but could not sing in the arranged key, and other times they would have no sheet music at all, but I was able to accommodate them in either case."

John began working the South Jersey seashore resort areas and spent ten years performing at venues from Atlantic City's Resorts International to important venues in Cape May, and every place in-between.

"I have never made a dollar any other way than playing piano and singing my songs - although I've done a few acting jobs when film companies would come to the Philly area. I've done some commercials and films, working through a casting director. I had a bit part in the film *Philadelphia* with Tom Hanks." John is now a member of the Screen Actors Guild and ASCAP. John is in his fifth year at his current engagement in the lounge at La Cena Restaurant (it means *The Supper*) in Bensalem, Pennsylvania.

I am kind of fortunate that I have a steady following. Some folks come to see me from as far away as Yonkers, above Manhattan, Allentown, and even further away. Philadelphia is, for me, a strong base of operation, where I have developed my vast repertoire."

With John's two great songs, "Saloon Song" and "Maybe Someday" gathering national attention, he feels he may now have a chance to move up the ladder, perhaps to garner engagements at New York's Cafe Carlyle, Tavern-On-The-Green, or at the Algonquin, or maybe Las Vegas, or even the Royal Room in Palm Beach, Florida, or some national festival concerts. "Maybe Someday" was featured on Dick Robinson's American Standards by the Sea, a nationally syndicated program. The song is a sort of sentimental sample of a time when popular music is what people listened to and enjoyed without the frenetic backgrounds and harsh lyrics of today.

"When I write a song, I usually have a particular performer in mind whom I would like to record the piece. I had Tony Bennett in mind when I wrote 'Saloon Song.'

"Someday I would like to step away from the piano and sing with a full blown orchestra. And I am working towards that goal right now."

John's influences were Frank Sinatra, Bobby Darin, and Tony Bennett. The composers he admires are pianist Peter Nero,

Henry Mancini and songwriter Burt Bacharach.

The world of today needs more saloon singers like John Primerano. He has the depth and the maturity of musical experience and the talent and the drive to complete his dream.

Many of today's talents that feature established music are marketed and their songs seem fabricated or sound like imitations of voices of past traditions in music. They do not introduce new, original material to continue the values of the music gone by. John Primerano is the real thing and you will be hearing more from him and his songs soon.

"No matter where I am playing, I imagine that I am on stage at a great Academy of Music, or at Carnegie Hall. I always thought the best compliment someone could bestow on a performer was that he always performed as a professional in his work. And that's how I have always tried to live my life."

Filippo Voltaggio

Filippo Voltaggio

He looks a bit like John Travolta, but the similarity ends there. Travolta acts. Voltaggio sings. He sings up a passionate storm of Italian Classics, and newer material as well. He is the everyman Italian crooner.

"Some may classify me as a sort of a tenor, but I am not. I wished I could be because my father was, but after so many years finding my own voice - being a baritone and being able to croon the songs I truly loved, I came into my own. My father was always interested in the high notes and whenever a tenor would hit a high note he hushed up the whole family so we could listen to it." Filippo's father didn't have much of an appreciation for the Frank Sinatra's and the Dean Martin's and didn't want his son to become a singer, mostly because he wasn't a tenor and was not able to hit those cherished high notes.

Filippo was born in Monterey, California with his parents both emigrating from Southern Sicily. As Filippo grew up and left his parents home he listened to the popular crooners we all know and found his own voice through them, as all emerging singers have done before him.

"The fact that there was always music in my home; my dad singing to records that were always playing, although it was mainly operatic arias, or pure Italian songs, it was in my blood. My father would teach me his Italian songs, as no one spoke English in my home until us kids started going to school. For us, everything was Italian."

It was Tony Bennett, Frank Sinatra, and Bobby Darin who mainly influenced Filippo in his quest to learn America's popular music. Italy's Dominico Moduno, of "Volare" fame, and Carlo Buti were far away influences as well.

"Although I mention the standard group of known singers, and even some not so well-known, I really grew up listening to them all, and because of my intense interest, they all influenced me in one way or another."

Being regularly in the midst of fellow performers, Filippo has crossed paths with his hero Tony Bennett, and Louis Prima's talented daughter, Lena, whose show he caught in a Milwaukee, Wisconsin performance at an Italian Festival, including Jerry Vale, Tony Orlando, and non-singing comedian Dom DeLuise, who worked regularly with Dean Martin, all working together at myriad Italian Festivals, where Filippo performs on a regular basis all over the country.

Filippo with Dom DeLuise 2004 (F. Voltaggio Collection)

The question of Filippo's unusual appearance with long blond hair prevailing beyond his shoulders came up during our conversation:

"I actually like my hair long, but was at one time worried about the effect it would have on my career. When I first started singing, the people that were hiring me were very concerned that it would be a problem for their audiences. When I got out into the audiences, it never, ever posed a problem. On the contrary, people remember me by my hair. So, I have thought about cutting it...and some day maybe I will."

Because of his appearance, Filippo has been likened to singer Michael Bolton and recording star Kenny G.

Filippo attended college, even studied vocalese and played roles in operas and operettas, became a serious engineer and found employment in junior management with corporate giant IBM. He nevertheless found time to audition to promote a possible future singing career, with auditions at the San Diego Opera and other spots, singing in the chorus, or wherever he could find work.

"At one point, I was at IBM listening to a broadcast on the radio of one of the productions I had done with the San Diego Opera. It inspired me enough that I had to leave IBM and pursue work as a vocalist. Friends questioned my decision, but, IBM, or any work other than performing, was not for me."

Filippo, with his cherished stories told when performing, or by his singing as a solo artist over the last few years, has accumulated legions of fans who seem to follow him. Becoming known as the ultimate performer, Filippo Voltaggio keeps climbing up the ladder.

"In my present goal as a performer, I would like to take that to the larger audiences, to people who have never experienced an all around performer on stage that can take you away for a moment and not just be in there dancing with murderous pyrotechnics and flashing lights, rather with a voice and a sincere story to tell."

Roberto Tirado, Jr.

Bob Tirado

It was a few short years ago that Roberto Tirado was a household name in the New York Metropolitan area. He was New York's Channel 11 and later Long Island News Channel 12's weatherman.

During those years, Bob, (commercially Roberto), appeared at community charity events singing the great standards. *Yes! Singing!* Then, during an appearance at the prestigious Tilles Center, Long Island's Carnegie Hall, entertainer, songwriter, and former "Tonight Show" Host Steve Allen, caught Roberto's performance, stepped backstage and congratulated him, saying, "Well, it was a pleasure to hear you sing so well."

That did it for Roberto. With that kind of encouragement, his singing career surfaced and he promptly recorded a great CD entitled *Prisoner of Love*, arranged and backed by the fine orchestra of Ben Grisafi. This anchorman, actor, producer, and Emmy-winning weatherman, can really sing.

Sounding a little bit like a cross between singer Billy Eckstine and Sergio Franchi, and sometimes evoking the smooth voice of Dick Haymes on one track alone, Roberto also rises to dramatic heights with Cole Porter's great standards "Begin the Beguine," (made famous by that Artie Shaw recording) and "Night and Day," done

Roberto Singing at Luisa Potenza's Italia Mia Luncheon, 2004
(M. Grudens Photo)

191

well by both Sinatra and Fred Astaire in past recordings, but, always a tough song to put over. And, a credit to his Italian heritage, Roberto sings the taunting "Mala Femmena," reflecting his feel and intense passion for lyrics.

"Like Sinatra, I truly *believe* the words of a song are as important as the music it supports." Roberto acts out the lyrics to make you believe them. "Otherwise," he says, "what is the point of interpreting a song?"

He emotionalizes every note. He entertains as he sings. He works the crowd well. Everybody knows him.

June 24, 2001

Dear Rich,

Thanks for your letter and the super review you gave of my new CD. It means a lot to me to hear that from you.

I listened to the CD by RobertoTirado. He's good! Thanks for sending it to me. Please tell him for me.

Keep in touch, friend.

Good luck and God bless,

Along the way, Roberto has received further encouragement. Legendary singer Frankie Laine recently wrote: "Roberto, I listened carefully to your new CD. You are good! So, keep going. Thanks for sending it to me. I started out a little late, but here I am. I made it. You will make it too."

Last year, Roberto performed to an

Max Wirz, Roberto Tirado and Richard Grudens, 2001

enthusiastic, standing room only performance in Smithtown, New York, backed by the Ben Grisafi Big Band. Ben, unfortunately for New York, has since moved his orchestra to Palm Beach, Florida, where he has been designated as the official Musical Director of the "Sally Bennett Big Band Hall of Fame and Museum."

Roberto performing with the Ben Grisafi Orchestra, 2003 (M. Grudens Photo)

Difficult as it is today to garner a recording contract for singing standards of yesteryear, Roberto is working on a new CD to be entitled *Flamingo*, a compendium of unusual, but tested tunes of the past, including that early thirties blockbuster evergreen recorded by Herb Jeffries with the early Duke Ellington Orchestra, "Flamingo."

Meanwhile, you can find Roberto performing in the New York area and on Long Island, where he has just completed engagements at the Stonybrook Cultural Center and on WALK radio, the *Italia Mia Radio Show* with Luisa Potenza.

$\mathcal{S}$ome $\mathcal{O}$ther $\mathcal{R}$ecent $\mathcal{C}$rooners

MICHAEL BUBLÉ *(Pronounced Boo-blay)*

Here is a twenty-five year old new guy on the block from British Columbia with Italian grandparents, naturally, who

encouraged his singing, Michael's voice is sometimes a dead ringer for Sinatra, and sometimes for Darin, although his voice is youthful sounding having not completely matured. I first noticed Michael when I heard and saw him singing while watching a televised ice skating event in early 2004.

Michael performed in the 2004 Super Bowl extravaganza along with Celine Dion and Shania Twain. Michael has the flair and penchant for becoming a full-blown star and seems to be a hard working and enthusiastic performer trying to make his way up the ladder.

"My Italian grandfather was my best friend when I was growing up. He encouraged me to sing. He wanted me to learn the songs he loved so much, music that has passed over my generation. Then I knew I wanted to become a singer and I knew this was the music that I wanted to sing."

When Michael sang "Mack the Knife" at the wedding of Prime Minister Brian Mulroney's daughter, he was noticed by producer David Foster of Warner Records who signed him with Reprise Records. Michael's rendition of "Moondance," "Come Fly with Me," "The Way You Look Tonight," and "How Can You Mend a Broken Heart" is proof enough of his star capabilities. His self titled thirteen selection CD is an indication that a star may be born as we listen.

Fortunately, Michael is a long way from his working days

at Chuck E. Cheese, and at work in a liquor store and light commercial fishing with his dad.

PETER CINCOTTI

Newer than new.

Peter Cincotti is just 20 years old. He sings like Sinatra.Or Bublé. Or Connick. Some say he is destined for the big-time. When still *very* young, he was exposed to jazz singer Ella Fitzgerald and big band leader and composer Duke Ellington. He began studying piano when he was three and started his vocals at fifteen.

Although he says he tries to stay away from songs beyond his years, he will eventually sing the appropriate standards, or, if they come his way, fresh and new songs that may become great songs. Piano wise, he follows his major influences Bill Evans and Oscar Peterson. He is graduating to the piano stylings of Nat "King" Cole, another worthy influence.

Because he is so young, it's virtually impossible for him to sing *mature* songs like" April in Paris," or "September of My Years," or even Ervin Drake's "It Was a Very Good Year," But he has great expectations and, as we all know, the years go by quickly.

Right now, Peter Cincotti is performing and touring when he can and garnering an education in-between. "I'm working with the Deans at school to determine the best way to handle my educational future. I am doing some traveling with respect to my performing now, but getting an education is just as important to me as my music." Peter Cincotti considers himself more a piano player than a singer. He prefers working in a trio setting. But his voice is rich and lush and will be an important adjunct to his career.

Peter has a new album out, *On the Moon*, with classic standards like "I Love Paris" and *South Pacific* wonder tune, one of my favorite Rodgers and Hammerstein songs, "Bali Ha'i," in a fresh, unusual version. It resonates throughout. On Concord Records. Peter is appearing in the new Bobby Darin Bio starring Kevin Spacey as Darin. The film is entitled "Beyond the Sea," also one of Darin's best records. You can also find him on the *Tonight Show* now and then.

TOM POSTILIO REVISITED

When Tom Postilio appeared in my first book, *The Best Damn Trumpet Player,* he was billed as the New Kid on the Bandstand-Sinatra Style. Tom Postilio is his real name, by the way. Tom was twenty-five at the time and we lunched in a cozy bistro named Sophie's in St. James, New York.

Tom had already been performing at the fabled Village Gate, at Eighty-Eight's, and the prestigious Rainbow Room at Rockefeller Center. During the Summer of 1995, Tom toured ten months with the world-famous Glenn Miller Orchestra and my pal, Larry O'Brien, the band's director, who, by the way, is still the leader. His debut album struck a familiar chord with the great standards, but with a new voice, and poignant moments of brilliance.

"I couldn't imagine doing anything else. When I am on stage I feel at home. I love what I do." Where have we heard that before? From Frank...from Tony Bennett? Of course!

Tom first fell in love with "our kind of music" when he was thirteen and had discovered his dad's archived Frank Sinatra albums.

"My interest grew out of a love for Frank Sinatra, whose music I love and when I began to sing, people actually began to compare me to him."

Soon, Tom realized he could not build a career on sounding

like Sinatra, so he began developing his own style, as others, who emulated Sinatra, had done before him. Before performing, Tom warms up by singing in the shower.

Tom with Richard Grudens

"And I hum, too! I've learned that a hot shower before singing is good for my throat."

Tom took three years of voice to learn the right way to vocalize. When he has the time, he opts for musical checkups. The eight month tour with the Glenn Miller Orchestra helped Tom

Tony Bennett and Tom Postilio (T. Postilio Photo)

strengthen song production in his earlier years. Concerts were held in small VFW Halls as well as the gigantic Hollywood Bowl with 18,000 in attendance.

"I was a little scared there, Richard, but now I go on more relaxed in my regular gigs like Vegas and Atlantic City. One of the natural hazards of the business is getting a little nervous before performances. They say it happens to everyone. You do pick up that extra energy - I go through jumping jacks to get the blood flowing."

Tom once met Sinatra:

"I really didn't 'meet' him. It was that I shook his hand for two seconds. But, it was kind of a weird, incredible feeling...like touching God! It was at Carnegie Hall in 1987. I couldn't believe his hand was so small......I don't know, it seemed unusual."

During my first interview with Tom in 1997, I asked him where he thought he would be by 2002 - five years later.

197

"I'd like to be where my friend Michael Feinstein is today - fairly secure and accepted in this industry. I wouldn't complain if I became a *Frank Sinatra* - like status, but that's pushing it to the highest. In five years I'd like to be closer to it. However, I have come to the realization that it won't happen overnight."

Well, Tom Postilio's albums speak of good material, good arranging, good backup. A solid sign of proper direction. No compromise on quality if lasting success is to be earned, something he understands clearly.

"That's a must. I am finding that young people are getting interested in the music too, and I credit Harry Connick, Jr. for that, even though he is not a romantic singer."

Tom does it all: He currently performs regularly at Rockefeller Center's Rainbow Room, proof that he is an accepted performer with a solid future. He is also booked often in the Oak Room at the Algonquin Hotel in New York, too. He really gets around, having appeared on cruise ships around the world, and in a number of "review" shows on Broadway, sings at New York City's Tavern -On-The-Green's Chestnut Room, at famed Westbury Music Fair on Long Island, where he carried his own concert in 2002, further enhanced by the 50 voice Hauppauge Children's Choir, and anywhere else he is called upon to lend his voice to gratified patrons of good music.

"I love the word 'crooner'. It's so evocative of that era with its great music and all the people who are my heroes. Sometimes I even think I don't belong in this age; that I should have been around

Tom Postilio
IN CONCERT

From Off-Broadway's Hit Musical, "Our Sinatra"

With guest star comedian
Angela LaGreca
from ABC-TV's "The View"

Friday
December 13, 2002
at 8pm

Westbury Music Fair

40, 50 years ago when pop music was music and not just noise as it is today."

TOM POSTILIO

Setting New Standards

The Oak Room

THE ALGONQUIN

Remo Capra Bloise

REMO CAPRA - A Rediscovery

Now, here is an Italian crooner, born in Bari, Italy, who is still making music, despite the fact that record producers are not currently issuing *our kind of music* on CDs. Remo Capra, a successful construction engineer who, by day, supervises rock blasting for the construction of some of the most prestigious buildings in New York City over many years, has performed with the great Louis Armstrong back in the fifties at Basin Street in New York when such jazz luminaries as trombonist Trummy Young, drummer Barrett Deems, and bassist Arvell Shaw played with the Armstrong All-Stars, and also sang with the original Tommy Dorsey band.

"I met Tommy Dorsey in New York and he introduced me to Tino Barzie, who eventually became my manager. Tommy heard me sing and invited me to sing with his orchestra on weekends. I loved singing and made records with Columbia, but my heart was divided, so I could not give up my engineering, which I also loved to do. If I made people happy by singing, that is fine. It is all possible if you like what you are doing. Besides, I like to be busy."

In 2001, coinciding with the publishing of his book *Bridge Over Niger*, and in coordination with Barnes & Noble, Sony released the albums "Just Say I Love Her" and "Say We Are Still Together," composed of the great standards crooned with a true Italian flavor, sandy but elegantly lilting voice; numbers like: "I've Got You Under My Skin," (recorded live at the Blue Note), "What Now My Love," (recorded in 1973 with Neal Hefti), "Passing By," (recorded in 1956 with Tommy Dorsey), and a good number of standards with conductor Frank DeVol recorded with Columbia in New York.

This is an enviable list of recordings and all done very nicely by a gentle and accomplished crooner who believes in the lyrics, as he sings them passionately and according to the lyrical requirement.

The book *Bridge Over Niger*, written with Pat Fahey, is

the true story of the simplicities and complexities of the structural engineering and completion of the strategic JFK Bridge that the United States built in 1970 for the Republic of Niger in West Africa, in which Remo was involved as one of its important paarticipants.

Remo once worked with composer Irving Berlin, obtaining permission to translate Berlin's song "How Deep is the Ocean" into Italian lyrics with nice results and is easy to listen to. You can find it on his album "Best American Love Songs in Italian and English" along with "As Time Goes By" and "The More I See You" with full orchestra and strings.

This man, who would not give up his career as an engineer, really captures the essence of all the great songs he has crooned over the years and right up into this new century.

REMO CAPRA
SAY WE ARE STILL TOGETHER

SAY WE ARE STILL TOGETHER
New York 2001 – Gato Barbieri on Sax
WHAT NOW MY LOVE
New York 1973
WINTER SONG (Solvej Song)
New York 1973
BUILDING THE RR TRACK
New York 1956 –
The Tommy Dorsey Orchestra
PASSING BY
New York 1956 –
The Tommy Dorsey Orchestra
I'VE GOT YOU UNDER MY SKIN
New York 1966 –
Live at the Club "Blue Note"

LA BELLE HISTOIRE D'AMOUR
New York 1966 –
Live at the Club "Blue Note"
JUST A MAN
New York 1985 –
Gato Barbieri on Sax
SHALOM & SALAAM (Song Of Peace)
New York 2001

LIVE AT THE BLUE NOTE:
PIANO: A. DONELIAN
BASS: D. JOHNSON

Sony Music
Special Products
AS 54659

This compilation ℗ 2001
Sony Music
Entertainment Inc.

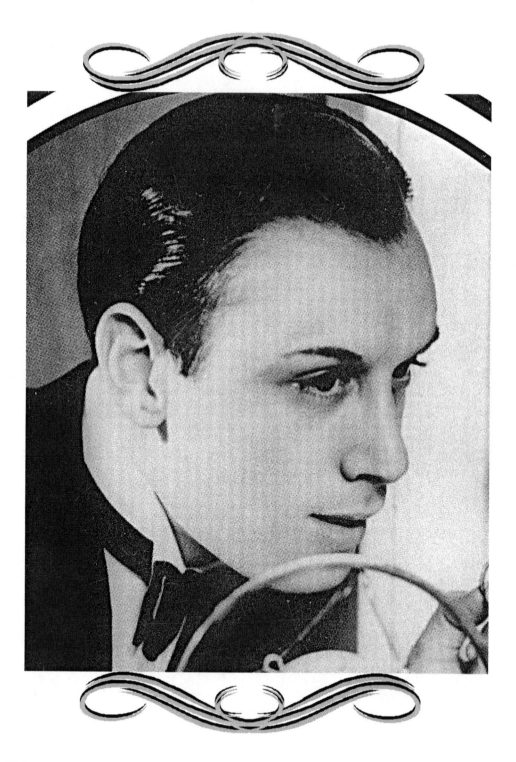

Ruggiero Eugenio De Rudolpho Columbo

Russ Columbo - A Career Cut Short

Bing Crosby spoke kindly of his rival Russ Columbo, the Camden, New Jersey born "Prisoner of Love" recording star of the 1930s: "I worked with Russ in 1930 at the Cocoanut Grove in Los Angeles. We were both working in the Gus Arnheim band. He played violin and accordion and sang. I just sang. I am sure if Russ had lived longer he would have been a big, big star. A talented and fine musician, he was a most attractive and appealing fellow."

Russ Columbo's baritone crooning style is sometimes mistaken for Bing's, as Bing was more widely known and people tend to forget the talents or even existence of Russ Columbo. Appearances at the famous Cocoanut Grove night club catapulted both Crosby and Columbo's aspiring careers higher. When Bing was late or didn't show up for his appearance, Arnheim would cue in Columbo to take his place for the bands vocals.

Within a short time, both he and Bing had their own competing radio programs. Russ on NBC and Bing on CBS. Coincidentally, both shows were scheduled on the same night and at the same time, inviting radio and newspaper columnists to inquire whether or not they were actually different people: "Are Columbo and Crosby one and the same?" one columnist wryly suggested.

On October 7, 1931, the *Hollywood Reporter* noted: *"Russ Columbo, former understudy of Bing Crosby in California, is a radio sensation in the East. While Columbo is cutting his wide swath, Crosby is beginning to fade."*

Newspaper reporters dreamed up a feud, calling it *The Battle of the Baritones,* but none existed. The singers actually admired and praised one another, and Russ was a guest of Bing's at his first son Gary's christening. Bing, although usually one to avoid such events, became a pallbearer at Russ Columbo's funeral.

There was much resemblance in their voices, delivery, and choices of material. Bing, however, generally performed brighter, lighter, richer, and more livelier - and at times, outright jazzy songs. Columbo's approach was more morose, serious, and sadder sounding. He sometimes blatantly imitated Bing and learned from watching him manage tricks on the microphone, using what he witnessed to his advantage. To most observers there was no mistake as to who was superior. It was clearly Bing. Both recorded "Prisoner of Love," "Out of Nowhere," "Sweet and Lovely," "Paradise," "Goodnight Sweetheart," and "Where the Blue of the Night," (which became Bing's theme) all being among the most popular songs of the moment. It was Russ who composed the sullen torch song "Prisoner of Love."

Russ was a child prodigy, an accomplished violin player by age five. He first played professionally at a theater in San Francisco at the age of thirteen and played violin in his high school orchestra in Los Angeles. In 1928, he joined the Gus Arnheim Orchestra after some playing experience at other ballrooms and dance pavilions in the Los Angeles area. In other work, his voice was substituted for actors who could not satisfactorily sing in films with Metro Goldwyn Mayer, a common problem in films at that time.

In 1931, Russ formed his own band and became a sensation with a more silky, ballad style of singing. One of the songs that heralded him was his own composition written with his manager and promoter, Con Conrad, "You Call It Madness (But I call It Love)." Russ toured the country and Europe singing "Prisoner of Love," "Paradise," "Auf Wiedersehn," and "Too Beautiful for Words," among others.

Russ appeared in a dozen films in his short career, including *Moulin Rouge, Wake Up and Dream, The Street Girl,* and *Broadway Through a Keyhole.* Russ also recorded with Jimmie Grier's fine orchestra. Early in 1934, Russ performed on his new NBC radio show from the Hollywood Roosevelt Hotel. His exciting, promising career, including his quest to become an operatic singer, came to a sudden end in a bizarre accident. On September 2, 1934, a close friend, photographer Lansing Brown, Jr., was showing him a pair of old dueling pistols at Lansing's home and struck a match to one of them that, unbeknownst to anyone, turned out to be loaded.

The gun discharged and Russ Columbo was struck in the eye by a ricocheting bullet. He was rushed to the hospital but did not survive. His death was officially listed as an *accident* by an official Court of Inquiry. Lansing Brown was crushed by his friend's death. Russ Columbo was twenty-six.

In 1936, closely following Crosby and Columbo, was singer Buddy Clark who sang in the same style and with the same Arnheim Orchestra. Buddy also possessed much promise as a popular vocalist, but, he too died accidentally, perishing in a plane crash while returning to Hollywood on a flight from San Francisco after attending a baseball game in 1949. He recorded a few Crosby-Columbo style tunes in the late thirties; "June in January," "Red Sails in the Sunset," and "With Every Breath I Take," and some popular tunes like Jack Lawrence's "Linda," "Peg of My Heart," and two duets with Doris Day; "Love Somebody" and "Baby, It's Cold Outside." He was thirty-eight.

Nevertheless, Russ Columbo had a brilliant, but shortened career. He will be remembered fondly by many.

James A. Durante

Jimmy Durante - *Everybody Wanted to Get Into the Act-and Jimmy Helped Them Do It.*

Jerry Vale loved "Ragtime" Jimmy Durante. So did everyone else. He had helped so many artists from Jimmy Roselli, Don Cornell, to Jerry Vale, through personal promotion and just offering old fashioned encouragement to his fellow performers, and going to bat for them when needed.

When Jerry was set to perform on the same bill as Jimmy, Jerry was to receive 100% star billing: "But, when I learned that Durante was placed on the same bill, I decided it would be okay to accept co-star billing. My co-star would be the great Durante. I've always admired him and was simply honored to appear on the same bill. We had great fun together and I'll always cherish my comradeship with Jimmy, who passed away a few, short years after our time together.

"I only wish everyone could have known him. A sweet man, a great performer, not just a relic of past vaudeville days, but a professional veteran who made it all look easy - stage presence, humbleness and honor among his fellow men."

Don Cornell always closed his concerts with a tune called "Old Man Time." "That song was given to me by my dear friend Jimmy Durante. My first job after leaving Sammy Kaye in 1950 was at Palumbo's in Philadelphia where I first appeared with him. On the third day he called me into his dressing room and said, "I have a song for you. I want you to take it and put it away and don't sing it for 40 years. 'You're too young to understand it now.' If you look at the lyrics you will understand what he was trying to tell me."

"He gives you youth and he steals it away,

He gives you nice pretty hair and turns it gray."

"Yes, I can only remember Jimmy Durante singing it, so I put it in my act. It's always a very personal experience each time I sing it, and the audiences adore it."

Jimmy Durante had established himself as the lovable comedian who coined comedy at his own expense after a long career in vaudeville. His prominent nose earned him the nickname "Schnozzola." Jimmy appeared in 25 movies in the 1930s including the film *Jumbo* in 1935, as well as many more later on. Even today, children know of him as the narrator of *Frosty the Snowman* which he did in 1969.

Jimmy was born in Brooklyn, New York in 1893 and passed on in Santa Monica, California in 1980 following a stellar show business career. His legendary songs, "Inka Dinka Do," "Young at Heart," "Start Off Each Day with a Song," "Did You Ever Have the Feelin'", "Hot Patatta," and "As Time Goes By."

Earlier, Jimmy was a hot piano player and bandleader, much influenced by ragtime pianist genius Scott Joplin. He performed in Coney Island, Brooklyn and in New York City. He played the piano at the Alamo in Harlem and assembled a group of New Orleans style musicians, billing themselves as Durante's Jazz and Novelty Band. By 1921, he became a renowned piano player and joined up with a music and comedy team called Clayton, Jackson and Durante, becoming regular performers on Broadway, Jimmy garnering a role in the play *Jumbo* which made him a full blown star.

In 1934, he composed and recorded what would become his signature song "Inka Dinka Do." Jimmy became one of the first television stars performing regularly on Milton Berle's *Texaco Star Theater*, where I first met him, and on the *Hollywood Palace* television show, and the 1950s TV variety show *The Colgate Comedy Hour*, alternating with other big time acts like Abbott & Costello, and Dean Martin and Jerry Lewis.

Jimmy Durante has shared the stage and camera with almost every known performer from Bob Hope and Bing Crosby to Frank Sinatra and Ethel Barrymore. He was the beloved Italian star of the Great White Way and every extension of show business that existed in his time.

The Lennon Sisters once told me that Jimmy Durante called them "The Lennon Goils." They loved it!

Jimmy usually signed off each show saying, "Good Night Mrs. Calabash, wherever you are." No one ever understood exactly what the meaning was for that famous phrase. Some have guessed the goodnight signoff was really a repeated melancholy goodbye to his late wife, Jeanne. Even his close friends only speculated. It remains a show business mystery.

Authors Choice - James Durante Album.

AS TIME GOES BY - The Best of Jimmy Durante - Mostly Recorded in the 1950s. There are 12 recordings. Songs included: "As Time Goes By," "September Song," "Smile," both heart wrenching, yet simple interpretations, "If I Had You," and "I'll See You in My Dreams." The latter is the song before he ends with a sweet goodnight to the ubiquitous "Mrs Calabash."

Lou Monte

A Treasure of Italian Novelties Everyone Loves

Famed for his cheerful and very Italian version of "Lazy Mary," Lou Monte has been a favorite Italian flavored singer with everyone since he came upon the scene in 1962 with this enjoyable melody originally composed by Paulo Citorello, with Lou's added lyrics:

LAZY MARY
Lune Mezza Mare
Lazy Mary you better get up
She answered back, "I am not able."
Lazy Mary you better get up
We need the sheets for the table
Lazy Mary you smoke in bed
There's only one man you should marry,
My advice to you would be Is to pay attention to me
You better marry a fireman he'll come and go,
Go and come sempr's la pompa a man tiene

C'e na luna mezza'o mare
Mammamiam'ho maritari
Figlia mia a cu t'ho dare?
Mama mia penscitu
Se ti piglia lu pisciaolo

Tssu vai, issu viene
Sempre lu peace a muno tiene
Se c'in gappa la fantasia ti pomperia figgiuzza mia
La lario la pisci fritt'e baccala
Oeh cumpa, na pompina ci haggia catta
Cenata o cumma ca mi voglio marita
Dammi na vagliotta ca mi voglio marita, HEY(repeat)

Some of Lou's other favorites were "The Italian Huckle Buck," "When I Hold You in My Arms" (Comm'a bella'a stagione), "Dominick the Donkey" (The Italian Christmas Song), "Please, Mr Columbus, Turn the Ship Around," and the most popular of all, "Pepino, the Italian Mouse," for which he earned a Gold Record.

Born in New Jersey on April 2, 1917, Lou Monte became popular with his versions of Italian peppered songs and made it big with the comedy classic "Pepino, the Italian Mouse" in 1962. You don't have to be Italian to enjoy this uplifting tune. Lou used to sing live on WAAT, New Jersey. Lou appeared on Ed Sullivan's famed television show countless times. He was the second performer on Frank Sinatra's fledgling Reprise Records. Sinatra was the first. Lou's recordings "I Really Don't Want to Know," and "She's An Old Fashioned Girl" proved that Lou Monte was not just a great Italian singer. I always enjoyed his rendition of "I Have An Angel in Heaven." Lou passed on too early in his life on June 12,1989.

Today, Lou's sons, Raymond and Ronald, have issued a CD of their father's Italian American character tunes laced with swing and jazz in the spirit of Louis Prima, who first pioneered this genre.

An afterword: Did you know that at every home game, the New York Mets Baseball Team plays at Shea Stadium, Lou Monte's recording of "Lazy Mary" is featured during the seventh inning stretch?

Honorable Mentions

This chapter will cover the activities of some other Italian crooners who established their vocal mark upon us during the musically enriched Golden Age of Music and beyond.

Giovanni Alfredo Desimons

Johnny Desmond

While in the service during World War II, twenty-one year old Johnny Desmond sent bandleader Glenn Miller a letter asking him to consider selecting him to sing in Glenn's Army Air Force Band. "The day I sent the letter to him he was building a band of good musicians to take overseas and form a great orchestra. He called for me and that was that.

"Under Glenn's guidance I developed a unique, personal vocal style that the fans really liked. That started off my long, fifty year career."

Giovanni Alfredo Desimons came to first light in Detroit, Michigan, studied at the city's Music Conservatory, and worked in local radio stations as an actor and singer. He organized a vocal group called the Downbeats which came to the attention of bandleader Bob Crosby, who hired them and changed their name to the Bob-O-Links.

Johnny sang with the group for a year and then with Gene Krupa's swinging band before his Glenn Miller days. After the war, he continued his career and signed with RCA Records.

A capable dancer, singer and piano player, he appeared with Barbra Streisand in *Funny Girl* on Broadway, and appeared at many Glenn Miller specials, tributes and reunions over the years. Johnny Desmond passed away in 1985.

Authors Choice Best Album

Vintage Jazz Band issued a compact classic VJB 1955-2 entitled Johnny Desmond- C'Est La Vie (That's Life) all classic Desmond material from his early period with MGM Records.

Alan Aldo Sigismondi

Alan Dale - Prince of Baritones

Alan was born in Brooklyn on July 9, 1925, the son of an Italian comedian who emigrated from the Italian provence of Abruzzi, and who had his own local radio show. Alan, from an early age, like many of his compatriot crooners, always wanted to sing. And he did so one night on his dad's show. That singular event eventually directed him to a life of singing.

While at Lafayette High School, he sang with local dance bands and at little places in Brooklyn's Coney Island. His first break was singing with piano playing band leader Carmen Cavallaro, who hired him to sing in 1943. He soon landed an extended engagement at New York City's Roseland Ballroom and quickly found himself in the recording studio singing "Every time We Say Goodbye" and "More and More."

Out on his own by 1946, Alan became a regular performer on the supper club circuit, and recorded his first hit, "Kate," on Bob Thiele's *Signature* Label, followed by a great rendition of "Oh! Marie." He went on to recorded forty-four songs with Signature Records. He had his own television show in 1948 on Dumont's Channel Five in New York, a show that was the first program to be *kinescoped* (electronically recorded) for national viewing. For Coral Records, Alan recorded "At the Darktown Strutters' Ball" with big band vocalist Connie Haines that became a hit for them both. He also recorded with fellow crooners Johnny Desmond, Don Cornell, and Buddy Greco.

In 1946, Alan amazingly led the fan-voted list of favorite singers on a WNEW radio survey conducted by the *Make Believe Ballroom* show hosted by legendary disk jockey Martin Block. When he recorded "There's No Tomorrow," (Tony Martin's signature song,) he segued into a chorus of the original version of that classic song "O Solo Mio," an established Italian melody.

Throughout the sixties and seventies, Alan maintained a very successful nightclub career and at such engagements as the Copacabana and Latin Quarter night clubs in New York.

Alan retired from show business in the late seventies. He had lost his heart for traveling from venue to venue. Throughout his career he was plagued by problems that included being blackballed by some television producers, and his resistance to cooperating with unsavory, controlling individuals who tried to manage him, curtailing myriad engagements

Alan always maintained a strong presence and independent lifestyle.

Alan Dale passed from us on April 20, 2002.

Authors Choice - Best Album

ALAN DALE Sweet & Gentle Crooner

Featured tunes: "Come Rain or Come Shine," "Cherry Pink and Apple Blossom White," "Night and Day," "Wrap Your Troubles in Dreams."

Scipione Mirabella

Skip" Nelson

When band vocalist Ray Eberle left Glenn Miller's band just before it disbanded, Skip Nelson, who also played piano and guitar in the band of Chico Marx, was recommended to Glenn by his old boss, Ben Pollack, and was fortunate to record with Glenn as a vocalist on two of the best Glenn Miller recordings, "That Old Black Magic," Skip's very first recording ever (in collaboration with the Modernaires) and "Dearly Beloved," the song that really showcased his singing talents; two recordings among the final recordings made for RCA Victor just in the nick of time before the infamous recording ban set in place by musicians chief, James Petrillo in

1942, a ban which would last twenty-eight months. With those two gems, Skip Nelson secured himself a permanent place in the charts of the world famous Glenn Miller Orchestra. When the Miller band disbanded in September of 1942, Skip Nelson took a job singing with his former boss, Chico Marx.

Carmen Lombardo

Carmen Lombardo - *Guy's Singing Brother*

Carmen Lombardo, bandleader Guy Lombardo's brother, band vocalist and musical partner for over fifty years, is best known for his world famous recording of "Boo-Hoo," a solid hit for the brothers back in 1937. It was the bands most successful recording, although "Auld Lang Syne," a non-vocal, is the band's theme. Carmen was the band's saxophone player and songwriter, as well, having written Arthur Godfrey's favorite tune, "Seems Like Old Times," and another hit tune, "Powder Your Face with Sunshine." The band moved from Canada to the United States and both brothers achieved everlasting fame through recordings and appearances.

Although, known best for his vocals with the band, Carmen Lombardo collaborated with a dozen well-known composers and lyricists on a number of tunes.

William Fiorelli

Bill Farrell -*Where there is Hope, there's Farrell.*

Big Bill Farrell is a product of Cleveland, Ohio. In 1947, at the night club *Chez Ami* in Buffalo, New York, Bob Hope walked in, liked what he heard, and took 19 year old vocalist Bill Farrell to Hollywood with his troupe. Bill signed to sing on Bob's radio show that also featured a youngster named Doris Day and Les Brown's Band of Renown. Bill traveled to Germany on the next Bob Hope USO Christmas Show. Bill would always sing with heart and soul: "I try to express a song the way I think a man would sing it," said Bill, who now lives in California and is singing better than ever.

Bill has performed at all the great venues, the Blue Note, Birdland, Copacabana; all in New York, and in Cleveland's Little Italy at the Italian Festival, and, of course, dozens of engagements everywhere. His current, yes, current, album, a CD named *With Love*, will be available. Music conductor Glen Osser, of Columbia Records fame who helped turn out many Jerry Vale albums over the years, organized and arranged his upcoming CD, yet untitled. Bill Farrell may be one of the most underrated vocalists ever. He still retains his deeply rich baritone voice.

Dominic Lucanese

Nick Lucas

A name, now not on anybody's lips, is that of Nick Lucas who was a popular guitar player and vocalist of the 1920s and '30s. Nick was billed as the "Singing Troubadour," Born in Newark, New Jersey, Nick and his brother Frank worked together. Nick sang and Frank played the ukulele. Nick found work at Pathe and played his original compositions, "Pickin' the Guitar," and "Teasin' the Frets."

In the 1950s, Nick toured Las Vegas, Reno, and Lake Tahoe, and was regularly featured on Ed Sullivan's television show. I think Nick recorded hundreds of tunes on Brunswick records. One of his best was "You're Driving Me Crazy," a tune he wrote himself:

You! You're driving me crazy!
What did I do? What did I do?
My tears for you make ev'rything hazy
Clouding the skies of blue.
How true were the friends who were near me
To cheer me, believe me they knew
But you, were the kind who would hurt me
Desert me, when I needed you
Yes, You - you're driving me crazy
What did I do to you.

Nick Lucas, who still retains a respective following passed away on July 28, 1982. He was eighty-five. Great Nick Lucas Brunswick records are "Blue Heaven," "A Cup of Coffee, a Sandwich, and You," and "In a Little Spanish Town."

219

𝒯he𝒥talian 𝔅andleaders
𝒜 𝒯ribute to the 𝒪ld and 𝒩ew

A Tribute

This, of course, is a book about the Italian *crooners*, who could not have prospered without the music provided by the bands who hired, spawned and accompanied them.

Italian bandleaders Joe Venuti, Guy Lombardo, Ray Anthony, Tony Pastor, Lee Castle (Castaldo), Jerry Gray, Buddy Moreno, Dick Stabile, Pat Longo, Henry Mancini, and Frank Sinatra Jr. and today's Ben Grisafi, Musical Director of the Sally Bennett *Big Band Hall of Fame* in Palm Beach, Florida, comprise the list of known current and past Italian bandleaders.

RAY ANTHONY

Ray Anthony got his important start in the fine orchestra of Glenn Miller up in the prestigious Cafe Rouge in New York where Glenn recorded much of his radio broadcasts. Ray states that

"Harry James is the best damn trumpet player," told to me during our interview in 1985 in New York. And, Ray is the logical successor to his mentor, that's for sure. And, today, he is still leading his own band, mostly at private parties, and selling tapes and CDs in his record distributing mail-order business.

Richard and Ray Anthony, 1989 (Camille Smith Photo)

Ray started at the age of five in the Antonini family in Bentlelyville, Pennsylvania, where his dad first taught him to play on the trumpet. Ray also credits Louis Armstrong and Roy Eldridge as influences. Generally a cocky guy in his youth, Ray went on to form his own dance band and toured the country featuring his own gutsy Harry James style of playing. His best-selling recordings of Dragnet and Peter Gunn television series themes are absolutely sensational. At one time, Ray had the number one band in the country.

Ray has been a bandleader, an actor, a television performer, and occasional stage actor, and now hangs out at the Playboy Mansion with cronies Hugh Hefner, Jerry Vale, Harvey Korman, Charles Durning, Chuck McCann and Sid Caesar, where they watch old movies and talk over old times over dinner. "All this is what keeps me young," he told me when I interviewed him for the Jerry Vale biography in 2002.

BEN GRISAFI

Being born and raised in an Italian house was all Ben Grisafi required to pursue a life of music. His parents had emigrated from the rocky hills of Caltabellotta, Sicily. Their love for Italian music nurtured Ben through the classic sounds of Enrico Caruso, Arturo Toscanini, and the great marching bands of John Philip Sousa, played incessantly and joyfully first on the family's windup *Victrola* record player.

From the time he was thirteen, Ben Grisafi practiced his saxophone and continued serious music studies. A few years later,

Ben Grisafi Big Band with Vocalist Denise Richards, 2004 (Bart Stevens Photo)

Ben would co-conduct the high school orchestra for an annual commencement exercise at the famed Brooklyn Academy of Music with his proud father sitting up front, a father who had once brought him to this very stage to see and hear performances of the powerful and influential operas *Tosca* and *Cavelleria Rusticana*, and now he had lived to witness his son conduct an orchestra before his very eyes.

A big band musician who once played with the likes of Billy Butterfield and other big bands, Ben Grisafi conducted the orchestra at Carnegie Hall, for an opening performance by Jerry Vale.

Now, with his own big band, and still performing in Palm Beach, Florida, Ben has turned out five memorable CDs on which he arranged, conducted, performed and has even composed some selections. These CDs are currently selling worldwide through Montpelier in England, and Ray Anthony's Record Sales in California, and are also obtainable on Ben's Website, *Ben Grisafi Big Band.com.*

GUY LOMBARDO

Guy Lombardo was originally from London, Ontario, Canada, born in 1902, and went on to become the most popular bandleader in America, selling at least 100 million records with his big band ensemble he named the *Royal Canadians*. The tag line was "The Sweetest Music This Side of Heaven." Between 1929 and 1952 there wasn't a year that a Lombardo recording didn't make the charts, with 21 recordings reaching #1. Guy's brother Carmen was

Guy Lombardo - (R. Grudens Collection)

the bands sax player and vocalist. Guy's addiction to a specific, non-changing musical style labeled the band as non-innovative group of musicians. His signature song, the Scottish anthem "Auld Lang Syne" that herald's in each successive New Year, is still played worldwide at the celebration of the New Year.

The Lombardo legacy of song includes "Seems Like Old Times," "Boo, Hoo," "Coquette," "Enjoy Yourself" (It's later than you think), "Everywhere You Go," and "You're Driving Me Crazy." The band also played for more Presidential Inaugural Balls than any other band of its time. Brothers Victor Lombardo and Lebert Lombardo also played with the band. Guy's Jones Beach Theatre productions on Long Island in the 1960s are legendary.

TONY PASTOR

An Artie Shaw protégé and sideman, Tony Pastor finally formed his own band when Artie suddenly left for Mexico and Tony's allegiances to Artie were over. A stellar saxophonist, Tony Pastor, under the same management as Glenn Miller and Woody Herman, began his career as a bandleader. His most famous vocalist, Rosemary Clooney recorded with him on a cute number called "Movie Tonight." Tony himself was a vocalist and had an engaging style.

During the 1940's my old friend Budd Johnson, whose career I showcased in my first book, *The Best Damn Trumpet Player*, enhanced the Pastor band by elevating its jazz content with his notable arrangements.

Tony's brother, Sal, played a very nice

Tony Pastor - (R. Grudens Collection)

trumpet style in a band that sustained itself into the late 50s. Tony's sons, Guy and Tony, Jr. sang with the band for awhile when Tony reduced the band to a small group and performed in Las Vegas. His youngest son at the time was Johnny Pastor who was a very fine flamenco guitarist. Tony Pastor's best were "A, You're Adorable," "I'm Confessin," and tunes like "Making Whoopee," and "Let's Do It," which he also vocalized in his impish way of performing a song.

LEE CASTLE

Lee Castle - (R. Grudens Collection)

I was introduced to Lee (Castaldo) Castle one day by vocalist Kay Starr in the 1980s at a gig in Huntington, New York. Lee had assumed the leadership of the Jimmy Dorsey Orchestra ghost band when Jimmy passed away in 1957. Lee had started his short-lived band in 1940, having previously played a distinguished trumpet in the organizations of Artie Shaw, Red Norvo, Tommy Dorsey and Jack Teagarden. Later he joined the combined Dorsey Brothers band in 1953, becoming the featured trumpet player.

JERRY GRAY (Genaro Graziano)

Jerry Gray, the great arranger of the Glenn Miller Orchestra in the early forties, first arranged for Artie Shaw. He was responsible for arranging Shaw's mega hit "Begin the Beguine," Glenn's "In the Mood," String of Pearls," the first Gold Record "Chattanooga Choo Choo," Pennsylvania 6-5000," and "Kalamazoo," among many others. Jerry composed

"String of Pearls," as well.

After Glenn disappeared, Jerry spent time with the André Kostelanetz Orchestra and then joined the American Band of the Expeditionary Force, Glenn's military band that served in England, and later in Europe. Jerry gave up his own large orchestra to spend time in Hollywood arranging for others. In the late sixties he reorganized his band and secured an engagement at the Fairmont Hotel in Dallas, Texas, and settled there until his passing in 1976. A sterling career, to say the least.

JOE VENUTI

Joe Venuti was a great jazz violinist who backed Bing Crosby, along with guitarist Eddie Lang, in their early days and eventually led his own orchestra Always doing pranks on stage, his antics were legendary. Kay Starr was his first singer. The band played during the 1940s and featured Barrett Deems, who became an important drummer with the Louis Armstrong Jazz players in later years.

Honorable Mentions are **Henry Mancini** of "Moon River" fame, who was originally an arranger for the Bob Crosby Orchestra, where he shared the writing with Paul Weston, Dean Kincaide and Ray Coniff, great arrangers all. **Phil Spitalny** and His All-Girl Orchestra that featured Evelyn and Her Magic Violin, **Luigi Romanelli** and his King Edward Hotel Orchestra in Canada. **Buddy Moreno**, a guitarist and vocalist who worked with Harry James as a featured vocalist, began his band in 1947, touring midwestern and southern states, settled in St.Louis and became the house band at the Chase Hotel and did a TV show on KMOX called the "Buddy Moreno Show." **Dick Stabile** started his first band in 1936 in New York. He had played with the *maestro* Ben Bernie and George Olsen's bands. A great sax player who could hit the high notes, Dick became Martin and Lewis' conductor and remained with Jerry Lewis after his split with Dean Martin and also performed in California at the Newporter Inn and at Ciro's nightclub, and in Las Vegas, eventually moving to New Orleans performing at the Fairmont Hotel. **Jack Fina,** formerly from Freddy Martin's band where he performed on the hit recording "Tonight We Love," Jack Fina led a small band for a while during the 1940s. **Muzzy Marcellino** first performed in the band of Ted Fio Rita who performed in films, and formed his own group in 1938, touring the west coast and occasionally in Las Vegas and Reno. He became associated with the *Art Linkletter Show* and remained for ninteen years until 1969 when he worked with small groups at private parties. Muzzy was a great whistler and made many commercials and performed in motion pictures.

Henry Mancini

Muzzy Marcellino

Jack Fina

Dick Stabile

Buddy Moreno

A Portrait of Italian Truths

This charming list of Italian truths will be understood by most Italians and those who are married to Italians and those of you who are friends of Italians.

Italians have a $40,000 kitchen, but use the $259.00 stove from Sears in the basement.

There is always some sort of religious statue in the hallway, living room, front porch and backyard.

A portrait of the Pope and Frank Sinatra hangs in the living room.

The living room is filled with old Bombonieri (they are too pretty to open) with poofy fancy bows and stale almonds.

God forbid if anyone ever attempts to eat Chef Boy-Ar-Dee, Franco-American, Ragu, Kraft, or anything else in a jar, box, or can. (Except Tomato Paste).

The following are Italian Holidays: 1st weekend in October-Grapes for the wine, and 3rd weekend in November - Tomatoes for the sauce.

Meatballs are made with pork, veal and beef. We are Italians, we don't care about cholesterol.

Turkey is served on Thanksgiving. That is, after the antipasto, manicotti, gnocchi and lasagna.

Sunday dinner was at 1:00. The meal goes like this: Table is set with everyday dishes...doesn't matter if they don't match..they're clean. All utensils go on the right side of the plate and the napkin on the left.

Put a clean kitchen towel at Nonno and Papa's plate. They don't use napkins.

Homemade wine and bottles of Seven-Up are on the table.

First course, antipasto...then change plates.

Next, macaroni (Nonna calls all spaghetti - *Macaroni*...change plates again. After that, roasted meats, roasted potatoes, overcooked vegetables. Change plates again.

Then, and only then (never at the beginning of the meal) may you eat salad with homemade oil and vinegar dressing only. Change plates.

Next, fruit and nuts - in their original shell only - but on paper plates because you ran out of dishes.

Coffee. Expresso for Nonno, "Merican " coffee for the rest of us, with Sambuca.

Hard cookies served to dip in the coffee.

Now, the kids go to play...the men go to lie down. They sleep so soundly you could perform brain surgery on them without anesthesia.

The women clean the kitchen. Nonna screams at them...half in Italian and half in English.

Italian mothers never threw a baseball in their life, but you can nail you in the head with a shoe thrown from the kitchen.

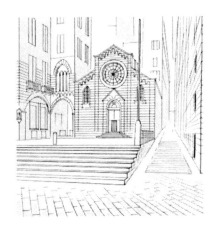

Radio Stations/Programs Playing Italian Music

New York Radio Stations

WALK	1370 AM Long Island	"Italia Mia" Host: Luisa Potenza	Sunday 11 a.m. to 1 p.m. (631) 955-1370
WHPC	90.3 FM Nassau	"Profumi D'Italia" Host: Rita Monte	Thursday 5 p.m. to Friday 3 a.m. (516) 572-7438
WRTN	93.5 FM New Rochelle	"Programma Ciao" Host: Dennis Nardone	Sunday 11 a.m. to 3 p.m. (914) 636-1460
WROC	90.3 FM Rochester	"Carosello Italiano" Host: Joseph Capogreco	Sunday 9 a.m. to 12 p.m. (585) 222-NEWS
WRUR	88.5 FM Rochester	"Italian Radio Program" Host: Giovanni Sebaste	Saturday 12 a.m. to 2 p.m.
WFBL	1390 AM Syracuse	"Music Italian Style" Host: Armond Magnarelli	Sunday 10 a.m. to 1 p.m. (315) 421-WFBL

Ohio Radio Stations

WELW	1330 AM Cleveland	"Touch of Italy" Host: Carmelina Antonelli	Sunday 12 p.m. to 12:30 p.m. (440) 942-WELW
WBBW	1240 AM Youngstown	"Italian Radio Show" Hosts: Little Joe, Joe Mazzocca & Phyllis	Sunday 9 a.m. to 12 p.m. (330) 782-1240

Pennsylvania Radio Stations

WEST	1400 AM Easton	"Tempo Italiano" Host: John Richetta	Sunday 9 a.m. to 3 p.m. (610) 258-9378
WPHT	1210 AM Philadelphia	"The Don Giovanni Show" Host: Don Giovanni	Saturday 6 p.m. to 7 p.m. (215) 839-1210

Rhode Island Radio Stations

WRIB	1220 Am Providence	"Voice of Italy" Host: Maria Gina Aiello	Sunday 10:30 a.m. to 1 p.m. (401) 434-0409

Texas Radio Stations

KTEP	88.5 FM El Paso	"Folk Fury" Host: Gregg Carthy	Saturday 7 p.m. to 10 p.m. (915) 880-KTEP

Canadian Radio Stations

CJVB	1470 AM Vancouver	"Radio Amici" Italian Language Broadcast Host: Maria Fierro	Monday to Thursday 7-8 p.m. Sunday 5-6 p.m. (604) 708-1234

CKJS	810 AM Winnipeg	"Radio Italia" Host: Carmine Coppola	Monday to Friday 5-6 p.m. (604) 708-1234
CFMB	1280 AM Montreal	"Radio Italiana Montreal" Host: Nino Di Stefano	Saturday 6 p.m. (514) 483-2362
Italian Radio			
Italy	Calabria	"Radio Valentina" Host: Frank Teti	radiovalentina@libero.it Phone: +39-0967-22116
Spanish Radio			
Spain	800 FM Cadiz	"La Otra Musica" Host: Jose Luis Bueno	tecomarsurcadiz@ono.com

About the Author

Richard Grudens of Stonybrook, New York, was initially influenced by Pulitzer Prize dramatist Robert Anderson; New York Herald Tribune columnist Will Cuppy; and detective/mystery novelist Dashiell Hammett, all whom he knew in his early years. Grudens worked his way up from studio page in NBC's studios in New York to news writer for radio news programs the *Bob and Ray Show* and *Today Show.*

Feature writing for Long Island PM Magazine (1980-86) led to his first book, *The Best Damn Trumpet Player - Memories of the Big Band Era.* He has written over 100 magazine articles on diverse subjects from interviews with legendary cowboy Gene Autry in *Wild West Magazine* in 1995 to a treatise on the Beach Boys in the *California Highway Patrol Magazine,* and countless articles on Bing Crosby, Bob Hope, including a major Hope cover article

Kathryn Crosby and Richard Grudens

covering Hope's famous wartime USO tours published in *World War II Magazine.*

He has written extensively about Henry Ford, VE Day, Motorcycle Helmet Safety, DNA History, among other subjects. His other books include *The Song Stars* -1997, *The Music Men* - 1998, *Jukebox Saturday Night* - 1999, *Snootie Little Cutie - The Connie Haines Story* - 2000, *Jerry Vale - A Singer's Life* - 2001, *The Spirit of Bob Hope* - 2002, *Bing Crosby-Crooner of the Century* - 2003 (which won the *Benjamin Franklin Award* for Biography-Publishers Marketing Association), and *Chattanooga Choo Choo - The Life and Times of the World Famous Glenn Miller Orchestra-*

2004.

Commenting about the book *Jukebox Saturday Night* in 1999, Kathryn (Mrs. Bing) Crosby wrote: "Richard Grudens is the musical historian of our time. Without him, the magic would be lost forever. We all owe him a debt that we can never repay."

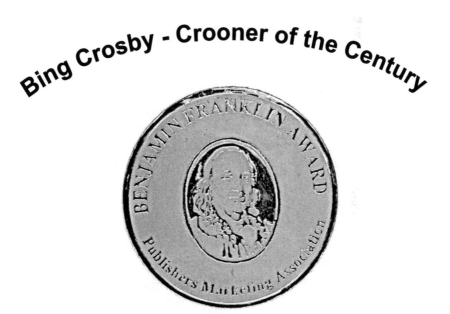

Winner of the
Benjamin Franklin Award - June 2004

Acknowledgments

When a book is born, the many individuals, all friends and compatriots, who participated in its formation must be acknowledged for their contributions, however great or small, as no one can fully create such a book alone.

This book is no exception.

First, my heart reaches out to **Frankie Laine**, my original mentor, for his encouragement from the beginning. And, next, to someone who became an inspiration in much of my recent work, the lovely and gracious **Kathryn Crosby**, who works tirelessly everyday traveling the world to insure and extend the legacy of her beloved husband, the one and only Bing Crosby, who started it all and thus, spawned a legion of followers, many who are subjects in this book and who openly acknowledge the fact.

Special thanks to the great **Jerry Vale**, who, after fifty-two successful concept albums still maintains a high place in the hallowed halls of quality popular music; **Connie Haines**, the living, loving legend song star who sang shoulder-to-shoulder with Frank Sinatra for three years and, later, worked shoulder-to-shoulder with me in my work; wondrous **Patty Andrews**, although absent in this tome, represents to me and the world, the powerhouse voice who unmistakably exemplifies the agelessness of our great music through the work of the great Andrews Sisters; **Larry O'Brien**, who diligently carries the torch of leading the great Glenn Miller Orchestra throughout the world; **Jack Ellsworth**, who continuously plays all the music we love over the airwaves and has, for over 50 years, on his daily program "Memories in Melody;" **Max Wirz**, a worthy partner who spreads the same joy to our European counterparts on radio EVIVA in Switzerland; **Jack Lebo**, who spreads the word in his own words throughout the country with his longtime column "Big Band Report;" **John Tumpak**, another expert of the big bands and their musicians who furnishes endless material through his interviews for all to read and enjoy; my dearly departed partners, photographer **C. Camille Smith**, to whom I'll always be grateful, and **Joe Pardee**, who was always there providing all the music help I ever needed.

Thanks go out to **Al Monroe**, New Jersey radio personality who contributes beyond the call of duty; **Jerry Fletcher**, who likewise sends contributions of music history accurately from his Florida home; Big Band leader **Ben Grisafi**, more a brother than friend; personal friends **Jerry Castleman**, **Bob Incogliato**, my son **Robert DeBetta**; and God's great gift to me, my lovely wife **Madeline Grudens**, who formulates, edits, provides photo assistance, and shares all the work that makes a book a book.

May God Bless them all.

Illustrations:

We extend a special thanks to the *Touring Club of Italy*. Editor Michele D'Innella of the Milano office graciously granted permission to incorporate the very fine landmark drawings of Antonello and Chiara Vincenti for use throughout the book in order to interject a true Italian flavor where it was needed.

Thanks also to Laura Albrecht for providing special Frank Sinatra photos submitted by Jean Albucci.

We are grateful to:

Madeline Grudens

Robert DeBetta

Ben Grisafi

Bob Incagliato

Luisa Potenza

Max Wirz

Jack Ellsworth

Jerry Fletcher

Jack Lebo

Jerry Castleman

Al Monroe

Camille Smith

236

Additional Titles by Richard Grudens
www.RichardGrudens.com
Explore the Golden Age of Music when the Big Bands and their vocalists reigned on the radio and all the great stages of America.

Chattanooga Choo Choo - The Life and Times of the World Famous Glenn Miller Orchestra

Commemorating the 100th Anniversary of Glenn Miller's life and the 60th Anniversary of his disappearance over the English Channel in late 1944, we present the tribute book Glenn Miller fans all over the world have been waiting for.

Bing Crosby - Crooner of the Century

Here is the quintessential Bing Crosby tribute, documenting the story of Crosby's colorful life, family, recordings, radio and television shows, and films; the amazing success story of a wondrous career that pioneered popular music spanning generations and inspiring countless followers.

The Spirit of Bob Hope:

Tracing Bob's charmed life from his early days in Cleveland to his worldwide fame earned in vaudeville, radio, television and films and his famous wartime travels for the USO unselfishly entertaining our troops. The best Bob Hope book with testimonials from his friends and a foreword by Jane Russell.

Jerry Vale - A Singer's Life

  The wondrous story of Jerry's life as a kid from teeming Bronx streets of the 1940s to his legendary appearances in the great theatrical venues of America and his three triumphant Carnegie Hall concerts, with appearances at New York's Copacabana, whose magnificent voice has beautifully interpreted the 20th Century's most beautiful love songs

Snootie Little Cutie - The Connie Haines Story

  The story of big band singer, Connie Haines, who sang shoulder to shoulder with Frank Sinatra in the bands of Harry James and Tommy Dorsey, and for years on the Abbott & Costello radio show, and who is still singing today.

Jukebox Saturday Night

  The final book in the series; interviews with Artie Shaw, Les Brown and Doris Day, Red Norvo, Les Paul, Carmel Quinn, stories about Glenn Miller and the Dorsey Brothers, songwriters Ervin Drake ("I Believe," "It was a Very Good Year,") and Jack Lawrence ("Linda," "Tenderly,") and a special about all the European bands past and present.

Sally Bennett's Magic Moments

This book is filled with extraordinary events in the life of Sally Bennett who established the Big Band Hall of Fame and Museum in West Palm Beach, Florida. Sally is a composer, musician, playwright, model, actress, poet, radio and TV personality and the author of the book *Sugar and Spice.*

by RICHARD GRUDENS

The Music Men

A Companion to "The Song Stars," about the great men singers with foreword by Bob Hope; interviews with Tony Martin, Don Cornell, Julius LaRosa, Jerry Vale, Joe Williams, Johnny Mathis, Al Martino, Guy Mitchell, Tex Beneke and others.

The Song Stars

A neat book about all the girl singers of the Big Band Era and beyond: Doris Day, Helen Forrest, Kitty Kallen, Rosemary Clooney, Jo Stafford, Connie Haines, Teresa Brewer, Patti Page and Helen O'Connell and many more.

The Best Damn Trumpet Player

Memories of the Big Band Era, interviews with Benny Goodman, Harry James, Woody Herman, Tony Bennett, Buddy Rich, Sarah Vaughan, Lionel Hampton, Frankie Laine, Patty Andrews and others.

240

Order Books On-line at:
www.RichardGrudens.com
Or Fax or Call Your Order in:
Celebrity Profiles Publishing
Div. Edison & Kellogg
Box 344, Stonybrook, New York 11790
Phone: (631) 862-8555 — Fax: (631) 862-0139
Email: celebpro4@aol.com

Title	Price	Qty:
The Best Damn Trumpet Player	$15.95	
The Song Stars	$17.95	
The Music Men	$17.95	
Jukebox Saturday Night	$17.95	
Magic Moments - The Sally Bennett Story	$17.95	
Snootie Little Cutie - Connie Haines Story	$17.95	
Jerry Vale - A Singer's Life	$19.95	
The Spirit of Bob Hope - One Hundred Years - One Million Laughs	$19.95	
Bing Crosby - Crooner of the Century **_Winner of the Benjamin Franklin Award 2004_**	$19.95	
Chattanooga Choo Choo The Life and Times of the World Famous Glenn Miller Orchestra	$21.95	
The Italian Crooners Bedside Companion	$21.95	
TOTALS		

Name:		
Address:		
City:	State:	Zip:

Include $4.00 for Priority Mail (2 days arrival time) for up to 2 books. Enclose check or money order. Order will be shipped immediately

FOR CREDIT CARDS, Please fill out below form completely:

Card #

Exp. Date:

Signature:

Card Type (Please Circle): Visa — Amex — Discover — Master Card

Italian Crooners Bibliography

Chintala, John. <u>Dean Martin-A Complete Guide to the Total Entertainer,</u> Exeter, Pennsylvania: Chi Productions. 1998.

D'Innella, Michele, Editor,<u> Italy, From the Italy Experts </u> Milano, Italy: Touring Club of Italy 2002.

Ellington, Edward Kennedy. <u>Music is My Mistress</u>. New York: Doubleday & Co., 1973.

Evanier, David, <u>Making the Wiseguys Weep-The Jimmy Roselli Story</u>. New York, New York: Farrar, Straus and Giroux, 1998.

Firestone, Ross. <u>Swing, Swing, Swing.</u> The Life and Times of Benny Goodman. New York, N.Y.: W.W. Norton & Company.1993.

Friedwald, Will. <u>Jazz Singing</u>. New York: Macmillan Publishing, 1992.

Grudens, Richard. <u>The Best Damn Trumpet Player</u>. Stonybrook, New York: Celebrity Profiles Publishing, 1997.

Grudens, Richard. <u>The Music Men.</u> Stonybrook, New York: Celebrity Profiles Publishing, Inc. 1998.

Grudens, Richard. <u>Jerry Vale- A Singer's Life.</u> Stonybrook, New York: Celebrity Profiles Publishing Inc. 2001.

Hale, Lee, with Richard Neely. <u>Backstage with the Dean Martin Show</u>. Los Angeles: California. Lee Hale Publications, 1999.

Kennedy, Don, and Hagan Williams. <u>Big Band Jump Newsletter</u>. Atlanta, Ga: Various Dates.

Laine, Frankie, with Joseph Laredo. <u>That Lucky Old Son.</u> Ventura, California: Pathfinder Publishing, 1993.

Lax, Roger & Frederick Smith. <u>The Great Song Thesaurus.</u> New York,N.Y. Oxford University Press 1984.

Lees, Gene. <u>Singers and the Song. </u>

Pleasants, Henry. The Great American Popular Singers. New York, N.Y.: Simon & Schuster, 1974.

Rockwell, John,. Sinatra-An American Classic. New York: Random House-Rolling Stone Press, 1999.

Whiting, Margaret, and Will Holt. It Might As Well Be Spring. New York: William Morrow & Co., 1987.

WNEW. Where the Melody Lingers On. New York: Nightingale Gordon, 1984

Index

A

Alberghetti, Anna Maria, 55, 99
Anthony, Ray, 59, 220, 222
Arlen, Harold, 84, 99, 177, 181
Arnheim, Gus, 205, 206
Astaire, Fred, 88, 89, 127, 192
Ayres, Mitchell, 65

B

B. (Babino), Tony, 2
Babino, Anthony, 173
Bailey, Mildred, 29, 87
Barzie,, Tino, 201
Basie, Count, 30, 41
Bennett, Sally, 193, 220
Bennett, Tony, 2, 3, 7, 25, 55, 58, 66, 79, 84, 85, 86, 87, 88, 89, 90, 94, 106, 107, 113, 123, 127, 141, 162, 163, 164, 166, 173, 174, 177, 184, 188, 196, x
Benny, Jack, 118, 159
Berg, Billy, 73, 74
Berle, Milton, 113, 210
Berlin, Irving, 84, 88, 181, 202
Bishop, Joey, 121
Bleyer, Archie, 94
Block, Martin, 215
Boone, Pat, 79
Boudac, Ray, 43
Bowes, Major, 21, 142
Brothers, Mills, 21
Brown, Lansing, 207
Brown, Les, 116, 217
Buble, Michael, 174

Burns, Ralph, 143
Butera, Sam, 43, 44, 49, 50
Buti, Carlo, 4, 11, 162, 188
Butterfield, Billy, 222

C

Caesar, Sid, 59, 221
Cahn, Sammy, 99, 181
Calloway, Cab, 42, 113
Cannatella, Ron, 47
Capra, Remo, 201
Carlone, Freddie, 63, 73, 107
Carmichael, Hoagy, 8, 73
Carroll, Diahann, 116, 127
Castle, Lee, 220
Cavallaro, Carmen, 215
Charles, Ray, 65, 88, 145
Cincotti, Peter, 3, 8, 174, 195
Clapton, Eric, 177
Clark, Buddy, 7, 60, 207
Clark, Dick, 79
Clooney, Rosemary, 26, 44, 55, 85, 89, 90, 94, 151, 223
Cole, Maria, 79, 183
Cole, Natalie, 177
Cole, Nat "King", 31, 152, 183, 195
Columbo, Russ, 2, 7, 58, 60, 67, 104, 125, 163, 205, 206, 207
Como, Perry, 2, 7, 8, 10, 54, 57, 63, 65, 66, 67, 68, 69, 73, 107, 113, 123, 125, 131, 144, 162, 163, 164, 165, 166, 173, x
Conrad, Con, 206
Coppola, Francis Ford, 134

Cornell, Don, 2, 7, 55, 57, 67, 103, 104, 108, 109, 125, 141, 162, 164, 165, 166, 173, 209, 215
Cornell, Iris, 107, 108, 110
Covington, Warren, 76
Crosby, Bing, 3, 7, 10, 21, 23, 41, 58, 64, 65, 67, 68, 104, 119, 121, 125, 157, 164, 170, 171, 173, 205, 211, 225
Crosby, Bob, 214, 225
Crosby, Kathryn, 157
Crow, Sheryl, 88

D

Dale, Alan, 2, 7, 105, 152, 215, 216, xi
Damone, Vic, 2, 3, 7, 65, 125, 127, 128, 163, 164, 165, 166, 173, xi
Darin, Bobby, 2, 7, 155, 156, 157, 163, 166, 174, 177, 184, 188, 196, xi
Darin, Dodd, 156
Davis, Jr., Sammy, 121, 159
Day, Doris, 7, 207, 217
De Lugg, Milton, 152
De Luise, Dom, 4, 117
Dee, Rolly, 44, 46, 50
Dee, Sandra, 156
Deems, Barrett, 201, 225
Desmond, Johnny, 2, 105, 152, 214, 215, xi
Di Florio III, Anthony, 141
Dickinson, Angie, 33, 66
Dion, Celine, 194
Domingo, Placido, 11
Dorsey, Jimmy, 76, 224
Dorsey, Tommy, 22, 23, 25, 27, 42, 49, 76, 173, 201, 224
Drake, Ervin, 17, 55, 74, 164, 183, 195